The Voice of the Phoenix Postwar Architecture in Germany John Burchard

THE VOICE
OF
THE PHOENIX

THE VOICE
OF
THE PHOENIX

Postwar Architecture
in Germany
John Burchard

The M.I.T. Press
Massachusetts Institute of Technology
Cambridge, Massachusetts, and London, England

To Margaret Clark Hopkins

Preface

This report was made possible by the Deutscher Akademischer Austauschdienst in Bad Godesberg, which offered me the opportunity to visit Germany extensively in the summer of 1963 and supplied generous travel funds, and the Carnegie Corporation of New York, which awarded me a grant for architectural and historical studies, of which this is the first slender fruit.

The German invitation I owe to the interest of Dr. Philipp Schmidt-Schlegel, at that time Consul General of the Federal Republic of Germany in Boston. Particular assistance was also rendered in the consulate by Dr. Gerhard Weber and Dr. Hermann von Richtofen.

In preparation for the trip, I consulted the conventional periodical sources and found three books particularly helpful, as follows:

G. E. Kidder-Smith, *New Churches of Europe* (New York: Holt, Rinehart, & Winston, 1964).
Rave and Knöfel, *Bauen seit 1900* (Frankfurt: verlag Ullstein Gmbh, 1963).
Alois Giefer, Franz F. Meyer, and Joachim Beinlich, *Planen und Bauen im neuen Deutschland* (Köln und Oplanden: Westdeutscher, 1960).

Almost every city has its own book and there are especially good ones for Cologne, Stuttgart, Mannheim, Hanover, Düsseldorf, Essen, and, of course, Berlin.

Most helpful advice and introductions were supplied by my friends, G. E. Kidder-Smith, Bradford Washburn, Jr., and Alvar Aalto.

German officials were universally courteous and helpful. Some went far beyond the call of duty and I should single out for special thanks in Mannheim, Herr Scherer, Verkehrsdirecktor of the Mannheim Verkehrsverein, and Herr Oberbaurat Dr. Schott; in Darmstadt, Frau Storer; in Cologne, Herr Dr. Zankl, Direktor Verkehrsamt, and Herr Volkmar Schultz; in Essen, Herr Dr. Lutscheidt,

Stadtoberamtmann and Frau Geberding-Wiese; in Hanover, Herr Lüben of Herr Dr. Hillebrecht's office; in Wolfsburg, Herr Dr. Hesse, Oberstadtdirektor, and Herr Dr. Gericke of the Press office in the Rathaus; and in Berlin, Herr Dipl. Ing. Rolf Schwedler, Senator für Bau- und Wohnungswesen, and Herr Persohn in his office. Herr Wingler of the Bauhaus Archiv in Darmstadt was a valued advisor.

On a trip and investigation of this sort it is particularly helpful to have the advice and guidance of architects, and those who were especially friendly and helpful include Helmut Striffler in Mannheim, Rudiger Thoma of the office of Hentrick and Petschnigg, and Paul Schneider-Esleben in Düsseldorf, Werner Ruhnau in Gelsenkirchen, Harald Deilmann in Münster and Fraülein Hetzold of his office there, Friedrich Wilhelm Kraemer in Brunswick, Dieter Oesterlen in Hanover, Hans Schädel in Würzburg, and Werner Düttman in Berlin. In Munich, Hamburg, and Stuttgart, due to absence or failures in communications, I had to fend for myself.

Collecting the photographs was certainly the hardest part of the task, and this mission was carried out faithfully, tenaciously, and skillfully by the staff of The M.I.T. Press.

The problem of telling the truth in architectural photography is a difficult one these days. On the one hand, few buildings now stand in serene parklike surroundings unchallenged by unsightly or incompatible buildings, untarnished by urban litter. This is part of the architectural ambiance, without doubt, but since we learn not to see it in life, photographs that emphasize it may well overstate the case for *Outrage*. On the other hand, architectural photographers with their cumulus clouds and dramatic trees may not tell the truth either. I have deliberately included some of each kind, and the careful viewer may indeed carry away an impression of how ugly man has made his city with his miserable poles and ash cans and street impediments, with his strewn papers, and above all with his automobiles. The photographs are of German situations; but their analogs can be found everywhere else.

I have used a few of my own photographs reluctantly and only when I could not lay hands on a good alternative. They lack the brilliance of many of the others, having been printed from color positive transparencies.

Finally, the manuscript was prepared for me in the first instance by my loyal associate of nearly forty years, Margaret Clark Hopkins, who died soon after she had completed it. As her last work with me I have dedicated it to her. She deserves a larger and better tribute.

JOHN BURCHARD

July 1965

Acknowledgments for the Photographs

Contents

Introduction

In the early summer of 1945, I made an extensive jeep tour of the American, French, and British zones of occupied Germany. I observed rubble from Munich to Bremen, from Aachen to Berlin. Eighteen years later, through a generous invitation from the Federal Republic, I had a chance to repeat the journey.

A trip through Germany today can offer a reflective American architect as much to ponder as the usual ecstatic visit to Philadelphia, New Haven, Täpiola, Vällingby, Ronchamp, Eveux-sur-Arbrêsle, Brasília, and Chandigarh, though of quite a different order, involving a consideration of the ultimate purposes of architecture often concealed in the brilliant cacophony of unusual forms.

This essay seeks to search the German achievement for examples that may help Americans with their perplexing architectural and urban renewal problems and to raise crucial questions concerning the motivations that produce great architecture and pleasant cities.

Can a society create outstanding architecture except for purposes that it holds to be genuinely important? The impressive German achievements in social architecture—housing, theaters, concert halls, recreational facilities—and in church building reveal what they value.

The Germans are actively concerned about the city as an urbane place. With respect to its greatest enemy, the automobile, the German decay is in an earlier stage than ours, but no more encouraging. Yet the prominent place given to civic music and theater, the zealous conservation of the city woods, the containment everywhere of extravagant heights all show that people can get or retain a good deal of urbanity if they want it enough.

The German efforts at reconstruction point up an array of questions directly relevant to our problems of urban renewal. To what extent should we restore or preserve old buildings? Should we try to rebuild old neighborhoods in the "spirit" of the admired past? When new buildings must be juxtaposed to old, what attention should we pay to the old? What is the role of memorials in our time?

It is not an easy task to preserve, even restore, the old while exulting in the new, and the Germans have not been wholly successful; but their efforts have been thoughtful and often noteworthy—in Bremen, Münster, Freiburg, and Hanover in particular—and I shall discuss them in detail. Considering these accomplishments, I find Ernesto Rogers' criticisms of contemporary Germany to be a limited observation of the totality of German work.

Germany, which bled itself of its own best architects, who went into exile during Naziism, has undoubtedly suffered from their absence, so that although a great many important international names were called on and produced good results in Berlin's "Interbau," this work lacks unified direction and is hardly the model of an organic quarter it was planned to be. On the other hand, the reconstruction of the center of Frankfurt, which was supposed to restore its courtly environment while respecting modern requirements, becomes despite the simultaneousness of its architectonic and urban character a phenomenon of a merely culturalistic nature. For the truth of an old environment cannot be repeated and the new requirements have not been expressed.[1]

The distinguished refugees Gropius and Mies have returned or are returning to build major works in Berlin; and unlike Rogers I cannot lightly dismiss the work of older men who stayed in Germany and did the best they could after fifteen years of repression, among them, Hans Scharoun, Otto Bartning, Rudolf Schwartz, and Dominikus Böhm. Moreover, a younger generation of eminent architects far outnumbers the roster of, say, Italy.[2] Germany lacks only the leadership of a world genius, although recent works by Le Corbusier, Aalto, Mies, and Gropius can be found there.

The German reconstruction also offers some comment on the consequences of haste. Naturally a people will be in a hurry to rebuild a country whose cities are more than half in ruins. The German rebuilding lay under relentless pressure of time; much had to be done posthaste; little seemed postponable. Materials were scarce in the beginning, and competent building craftsmen as well. The consequences of this are sometimes all too evident. That they were not inevitable in all situations is demonstrated by the beautiful Notkirchen built in many parts of Germany by Otto Bartning in the late forties and early fifties, using the simplest materials and the most primitive means. Not all the speed may have been necessary. Do we, without the same justification, need to act in equal haste? Are we even compulsive about the creation of rubble in the name of urban redevelopment before we are dead sure what we will build on the ruins? Even a phoenix may need a certain period of gestation.

The new German scene suffers from having been created in a short span of years and thus presents an overconcentration of what was current and choice at a given moment in time. The trouble is that what was current in 1950 was not very choice so that the urbanity, say, of London's anonymous Georgian squares or the Palais Royal and the Place des Vosges in Paris is entirely missing. And the results are not quite unobtrusive enough to serve as curtains against which more brilliant individual achievements can be displayed.

[1] Ernesto N. Rogers, "The Phenomenology of European Architecture," *Daedalus,* Winter 1964, p. 370.

[2] A partial German list would include Paul Baumgarten (Berlin), Harald Deilmann (Münster), Werner Düttman (Berlin), Wils Ebert (Berlin), Egon Eiermann (Karlsruhe), Rolf Gutbrod (Stuttgart), Helmut Hentrich (Düsseldorf), Bernhard Hermkes (Hamburg), Friedrich Wilhelm Kraemer (Brunswick), Dieter Oesterlen (Hanover), Werner Ruhnau (Gelsenkirchen), Paul Schneider-Esleben (Düsseldorf), and others whose names will appear here and there in the text.

Finally, many German architects in the postwar period have made the same serious attempt to join the other arts to architecture as have a number of Americans. The range of results in Germany is considerable, and a special section is devoted to this aspect of architecture.

There are flaws in the German accomplishment, but these are not the main interest of this study. I want to stress instead that the stereotyped judgments on the quality of German architecture, past and present, may be unfair. We can learn from its successes as well as its failures.

As I looked at the Federal Republic of Germany in 1963, it was hard for me to remember the devastation I had noted in 1945. German books do not quite tell the story, either. It is thus easy to underrate the magnificence of the rebuilding, measured as sheer effort. No matter what the source of funds, no matter what the aid, there have been few material achievements to match it.

Of the eleven million people who inhabited the ten largest cities in 1939, almost six million were bombed out, mostly in 1944 and 1945. The percentage of the city destroyed varied from a minimum of 40 in Munich to a maximum of 72 in Cologne with the median near to 60. The Germans had to deal with some three hundred million cubic yards of rubble, equivalent to the volume of three hundred Empire State Buildings or one hundred Pyramids as large as the Great Pyramid of Cheops. The rubble would have provided material for a wall four feet thick and eight feet high around the entire United States, four feet thick and eighteen feet high around the old European boundaries of Imperial Germany, or six feet thick and twenty feet high around the perimeter of the new Federal Republic. From it the Berliners built whole new hills, the Hanoverians the base for an enormous new stadium.

The situation varied little from city to city. One dwelling in three was left standing in Stuttgart. Darmstadt was 70 per cent destroyed. Of Hanover's 150,000 houses, one half were completely destroyed, another 40 per cent damaged. Her population of 473,000 in 1939 had dropped to 217,000 by 1945. Two thirds of the houses in Münster were leveled, while only 3 per cent of her apartments remained intact. The 1939 population of 132,000 had dwindled to 25,000 by 1945 (it is now 185,000). These figures are characteristic.

It is easiest to talk statistically in terms of housing units, but almost everything else went too: ancient and loved landmarks, utilitarian buildings of all kinds, churches and factories, hospitals and theaters, office buildings and schools; in cities like Berlin even the trees, which are hardest to restore in a hurry (there are 225,000 young trees on Berlin streets today). So a great deal of the Federal Republic of 1964 has been built in the last fifteen years, although a visitor may be deceived now and then by some skillful restorations.

Berlin's recovery is the most noticeable partly for ideological reasons and partly because there are still so many open lots to remind the visitor of 1945. There are such lots in Munich too but with no such dramatically juxtaposed new constructions. The Berlin result is noticeable on an absolute as well as on a relative scale. Its construction volume costing 470 million DM in 1949 rose with only occasional sags in the curve, notably in 1952, to 1,300 million DM in 1962. The equivalent dollars, which amount to about 120 million in 1949 and 325 million in 1962 tend to understate the quantitative achievement to us who might see more dollars than that in standing jet transports at O'Hare field every hour. Every fourth Berliner of today lives in a new flat. The school system has been essentially rebuilt, from the 2,346 classrooms remaining to 7,578 in 1962; the technical university enlarged and modernized; the Charlottenburg university largely replaced; a new "Free University" built in Dahlem. There are a new opera house and a new concert hall, a new building for the Academy of Arts, a new and refurbished zoo, several good theaters; there has been almost a complete rebuilding of churches; the old hotels have been restored and two big new ones built; there are 618 new sports grounds and playgrounds; there is a congeries of large new commercial buildings around the Ernst Reuter Platz; the subway has many excellent new lines and stations; there are 118 new bridges since the blockade, 150 new miles of bicycle paths, and a big start on a belt highway system. There are 86 new day nurseries, 22 new homes for the aged, 2,000 new hospital beds. *Mutatis mutandis* comparable things have happened in almost every other important West German city except perhaps Nuremberg and Munich.

All this achievement is not less than fabulous in purely materialistic terms.[3] You have only to cross the Rhine into France to feel the difference. But the German accomplishment also puts the quality of work in Italy or England well in the shadow. The achievement comprises striking examples of almost universal competitions for important buildings which usually have included meeting a budget in order to qualify for the first award; a fine demonstration of sobriety in the first postwar years (just as in Italy, brought about I suppose by a combination of embarrassment, contrition, and plain lack of means) coupled with an emergence from that sobriety along reasonable grounds, seldom bursting into eccentricity as was so often the case in Italy; an example of enormous respect and love for the past together with a will to do today's task in today's terms; and as might be expected most efficient organizational powers (although it has to be reported that the myth that every German always meets his appointments with almost offensive punctuality is not based on much fact).

[3] An extended discussion of the quantitative achievement together with an analysis of the economic, political, and administrative mobilization which made it possible would be useful to have. I hope someone will provide it.

German Architectural Education, Practice, and Attitudes toward the Eccentric

A little needs to be said about the way German architects are trained, the way they work, and the general consequence of this.

It is hard to be complacent about our architectural education compared with what is now going on in Germany. Architects there have a far more serious grounding in engineering and science; they understand construction better; the schools at Stuttgart, Brunswick, and Berlin, at least, are working on a deeper integration of city planning and design and architecture than has even been begun here except in a verbal way. But the most striking thing is the relation of the leading architects to the schools: Most of them are genuine working professors while carrying on practices which are rewarding enough, too. (Of course German architects have been spared the distinction of being world travelers and affluent big businessmen.) I compiled a list of the leading contemporary German architects which added up to forty-three. Of these, twenty-four were practicing professors and eight more were city baumeisters, which implies in part another kind of teaching. Only eleven were engaged in exclusively private practice and perhaps not more than five of these were among the best known. The teaching arrangement is not like ours since it demands more independence in the student, but the teaching responsibilities cannot be discharged by casual, short, and unprepared visits or by mere attendance at juries. It is also expected that every student will experience strong and different talents (thus Oesterlen and Kraemer at Brunswick; Gutbrod and Deilmann, commuting from Münster, at Stuttgart, and so on).

If we wish to contrast this situation with that in America, we might start by putting together a list of the same number of leading architects. I found I was easily able to accommodate in such a number all the big names, all the more than local-medium names, the way-outs and the sober, and all the leading large firms, whether or not distinguished. Of the forty-three Americans I can count fourteen who are or have been clearly connected with education. Of the fourteen, eight once had strong connections but have them no longer. Of the remaining six, all eminent, perhaps a few might be said to be "working stiffs" like Kahn, Thompson, and Rapson, while the others are at best mere prestige-shedders of which our architectural education needs no more. Thus the German ratio is at the least three fifths teaching, the American at best one seventh. I firmly believe that this situation will in the end have important consequences. We no longer have a situation where theorist-teachers of the type of the French school abound or are wanted (though in their best days they were effective); we have found no way to connect our most talented architects with the teaching process, at least not before the students begin their internship in somebody's office where undoubtedly a good deal of education goes on. Education as a form of apprenticeship will, I should think, pay off for German architecture in the long run, as, I think, barring major reforms equal to those of the Bauhaus, our present system may mar architecture in America.[4]

It is interesting to note that the characteristically small offices of the Continent have spawned fewer personality cults than have arisen in the United States with its greater degree of apparent organization. One could say, that this was because the Europeans save for Le Corbusier and Aalto, and more particularly the Germans, had failed to provide the personalities around which cults could form. I believe this to be categorically untrue, that the work of many European architects is quite the equal of the work of a number of Americans about whom so much local fuss is made.

On the other hand, one might explain the Kahns, the Soleris, the Lundys, and maybe even the Rudolphs as refugees from the American way of doing architectural business were it not for the fact that other self-conscious American form makers do operate very much in the American way and with what would seem in Germany to be enormous organizations.

There is at least a mild sickness in a system which regards every new building as a potential seven days' wonder; it is a disease which infects students and the architects who need to be admired. If allowed to wax, it may yet make architects into milliners. Whether it is a consequence of the generally inferior quality of American architectural journalism as compared with that of England, Italy, Japan, and other countries is not certain; the journalism may on the other hand be the consequence of architectural attitudinizing rather than the promoter of it. Whatever be the reason, there is less of this to be found in Germany.

Yet one would expect that the near universality of competitions for important German buildings would incite greater diversity since to be unusual is a good way to survive to the final judgment with many juries, German or American. Jurors are after all human, with their prejudices and predilections, and those who do so much judging as almost to have made it a profession may find that their jaded taste needs stimulation which only the unusual can provide. German jurors and German architects may be more sober than their American counterparts, to be sure. Clearly German publicity is more sedate and there is less to be gained by the architect who guns for the headlines. The critics are fewer, better trained, and more serious, so all together there is less cocktail-party chat about architecture. Moreover the conditions of the competi-

<hr />

[4] The only reservation about this is the sobering one that many of the architects of today whom we most approve are products of academies whose methods we wholeheartedly disapprove. But this demands a different essay.

tions help to explain the absence of any very dramatic eccentricity.

In Germany there are competitions for almost every important building, public or private. Alvar Aalto was directly commissioned for the Kulturzentrum and the church in Wolfsburg, but this was unusual, and he had to win the competition for an opera house in Essen.

The competitions may be open or invited. An important detail is that in most cases one of the conditions involves the estimated cost of the building. A design which flagrantly ignores this consideration and is far over the budget may be very exciting and may win some aesthetic praise for its designer, but it will not win him the commission. This has happened to the brilliant Hans Scharoun on more than one occasion. In any event such rules tend to restrain the wildest ideas. Whether this is good or bad may depend upon one's point of view.

Perhaps the more careful training of the German architects results in a more restrained attitude with respect to innovations, sometimes too restrained. One cannot say that there are no strange buildings in Germany, but it is harder to find an interesting cluster of eccentricities there than it is here. One can think of a few places where the postwar sobriety has been shattered. Indeed, the sobriety was surely in part not a matter of choice but instigated by poverty of money and materials, necessity for rapid utilitarian rebuilding, the emigration or exile of some (though not all) of the potential innovators, and the reminiscences of the Nazi neoclassic which some thought could perhaps be purged of its connotations if it were simplified and shorn of its monumental elements. There may have been also some mystique of atonement through modesty such as some Italian critics think underlay the first postwar Italian architecture. Too many buildings may have been controlled by the bureaus. Whatever the cause, the result is a large number of workable, not very noticeable buildings from the early years, neither ugly nor beautiful. They might conceivably have served as an anonymous backdrop for more exciting things, but they were not so arranged on the city plan. Their over-all design was generally quiet, but their fenestration often assertive. Examples can be found at random in any German city. Entirely characteristic are the AEG-Verwaltungsgebäude by Fritz Krudt in Essen in 1952, a horizontal building, or W. M. Schneider's Allbauhaus on the Salzmarkt, also in Essen, a tall one. Even architects who would later do work of personal distinction were involved, as Dieter Oesterlen when he designed the Arbeitsamt on the Clevertor in Hanover of 1950. The buildings might be done here and there with a little more variety and distinction, such as Dustmann's Niedersächsische Landesbank of 1956 in Hanover. By 1957 the style was developing and improving; an example is Friedrich Bauer's Central Post Office on the Paradeplatz in Mannheim; or in a different direction with more emphasis on spandrels and masonry, Hans Mehrtens' Bergbau-Forschungsanstalt, also of 1957, in Essen. But the differences between such buildings to the passing eye is slight indeed; none is memorable; and the first impression is of a Germany with a monotonous style of which the examples could be multiplied indefinitely, if not very well recalled. Bonn abounds in buildings like Franz Meyer's Ministry of Finance; Frankfurt is full of respectable nonentities such as the Federal Audit Office by Friedel Steinmeyer and Werner Dierschke. There are many in Hanover that resemble Prendel's Niedersächsisches Department of Welfare. These are not all buildings for bureaus of government; similar designs can be found among the early schools, hospitals, and private office buildings as well.

This work is an unhappy reminder of what be-

1
Hanover. Niedersächsische
Landesbank, Georgplatz.
Professor Dustmann

2
Mannheim. Main Post
Office, Paradeplatz.
Friedrich Bauer

gan to develop later among American architects as they first attempted to exploit precast concrete. Such trends here and in Germany offer reminiscences of the earlier ubiquity of the unlamented cast-iron style of our mid-nineteenth century. Nonetheless, the first encounter with it in Germany may be favorable, as a sort of reaction against the excessive amount of innovation, or at least at efforts to be different, among American architects, even very good ones who ought to know better. In America more than any other country architects are at once the victims and the abettors of the clacking tongues of critics and tastemakers and "in" groups. Nothing remains "the thing" very long, and it is easy even for great men to be considered old hat while the pursuit of the latest Wunderkind and the excessive presentation of him when found is a daily occurrence.

It happens in all the arts, of course, and it happens to some degree in every country. Hannah Ahrendt described it well in her review of the novel *The Golden Fruits:*

The falsity of the intellectual "they" is particularly painful, because it touches one of the most delicate and, at the same time, indispensable elements of human relationships, the element of common taste for which, indeed, no "criterion of values" exists. Taste decides not only about how the world should look, it also determines the "elective affinities" of those who belong together in it. . . . This feeling of natural kinship in the midst of a world, to which we all come as strangers, is monstrously distorted in the society of the "refined" who have made passwords and talismans, means of social organization, out of a common world of objects.[5]

But it is an unstable world, made less stable by the journalists' insatiable appetite for novelty.

There are other equally restrictive canons of taste in Europe, of course, notably the develop-

[5] Hannah Ahrendt, Review of *The Golden Fruits* in *The New York Review*, Vol. II, No. 2 (March 5, 1964), p. 6.

ment of magazines which stick loyally, à la CIAM, to one clique or another, and this may have equally bad effects if one leans only on the pronouncements of one journal or group. Yet there is at least a certain stability of consistency inside each partisan group which up to now has been missing here.

In German churches and theaters especially and in a more modest way in the housing, one finds a number of personal and fine buildings which nonetheless can be excluded from the roster of the eccentric, and of these I shall have more to say later. Perhaps some people would class all of Hans Scharoun's work as eccentric, but I do not feel that way about either the Philharmonic in Berlin or his latest housing there, or the Romeo und Julia apartments in Stuttgart, or the Geschwister-Schule in Lünen.

Unusual, eccentric if you will, but brilliantly effective are Bernhard Hermkes' greenhouses in the Planten un Blomen in Hamburg. This whole park is a great delight, a large and charming place to walk and rest and examine flowers even when the great international shows are not there, even when the *téléfériques* are not conveying passengers from one end of the grounds to another. The layout is one which might have given the designers of New York's Fair an idea or two if they ever had time or inclination to contemplate a quiet idea. Anyway, among the fine things in this park Hermkes' greenhouses stand high. At first glance they may seem only like some eccentric and unnecessarily dramatic arrangements of steel trusses and other structures to support greenhouse glass. But they are much more, as one soon realizes. The visitors have to pass through many experiences as they view this splendid array of plants out of the weather but under the various conditions of humidity and aridity, sun and shade, heat and cold, terrains where the ceiling should be close and others where it must be high. All this, and the cir-

3
Hamburg. Federal
Gardening Exhibition,
Planten un Blomen.
Bernhard Hermkes

culation through the complex, the architect has conceived with sensitivity and skill, both inside and out. Inside, as is proper, the eye is concerned with the plants; outside the forms mount above the terraces and the pools and the Henry Moore sculpture, pausing to form walls for this terrace and standing aloof from another. This Hamburg achievement is extraordinary even in comparison with Joseph Murphy's excellent botanical dome in St. Louis, limited as it is by the inflexibility of Buckminster Fuller's tetrahedral ideology. There are other good examples of this German skill, including the fine new house in Berlin where birds of exotic plumage fly free above one's head and light in appropriate foliage. Why do the Germans do these things well? It is not a matter merely of architectural skill, I suggest. Americans go to zoos only then they are young, when their children are young, and when their grandchildren are young. The Germans go in between as a serious exercise in educative pleasure, just as they go to gardens. And though there are some ways in which German taste may be inferior to ours, it does not tolerate the confused notions about the animal and vegetable worlds implicit in the cult of Mickey Mouse, Donald Duck, or the still more offensive bland and nameless chipmunks that are whistling metaphorically in every nook and cranny of Disneyland.

Other eccentricities of Hermkes are less successful; for example, the Phillips tower in the same park or his Auditorium Maximum at the University of Hamburg.

Another man to whom more than passing attention needs to be paid and who could be classed as eccentric is Werner Ruhnau of Gelsenkirchen. Of his realized work the most familiar is the unusual and successful theater at Gelsenkirchen. He is dedicated in theory and practice to the idea of achieving sooner or later as technique and habits permit the freest possible architecture, where roofs might be replaced by horizontal air pressure and climatizing achieved by radiation and "corrected atmosphere." It was in this pursuit that he made his proposals for a theater in the ruins of the Stiftskirche in Bad Hersfeld, an open-air theater to be operable even when the weather was bad. On a less spectacular but still advanced level, he has tried to go beyond the "total theater" of Gropius and Piscator, the globular theater of Weininger, the theater with removable walls of Clemens, the arena stage of Mies and others. He seeks to remove *all* the walls of the theater so that the stage manager may be able to construct the room he wants for each performance: "the floor moves evenly over stage and auditorium, thus enabling everywhere the constructions of mounds and hills." [6] Such freedom also should permit the baroque "vis-à-vis" theater or any other kind of desired seclusion. He pushes the theory to its ultimate conclusion, which may or may not be a reduction to absurdity. If the stage and the auditorium should not be separated areas any more, neither should the theater and the town landscape. This was the theory which produced Emanuel Lindner's sketch for the Opera House, Essen, a competition in which Alvar Aalto was the winner. To what extent Ruhnau has thus far been able to realize his theories is demonstrated by the theater in Gelsenkirchen.

But the consequences of an application of Ruhnau's theories no doubt prevent their adoption by American architects, whether or not they are form makers. Consider his own words:

The modern, changeable, and open architectures demand an active and open person. Personal liberty is a shallow word only unless society and its architectures enable the possibilities of personal activity. Therefore modern

[6] Private communications to the author from Werner Ruhnau, attached to copy of *Architekt Werner Ruhnau und seine Konzeption,* brochure published by Alfred Marschall, Munich, December 1960, n.p.

architectures have to be fluent, movable, and indeterminate as to their forms. The people using them must be the elements themselves to determine the form. . . . Architecture becomes self-absorbed as a determining fact as to form in order to open for the users the greatest possible liberties.[7]

However practical or impractical this may be, it poses the issue clearly between those who would extrapolate the earlier simpler ideas of Mies and Gropius and those who follow the old paths of Wright, Le Corbusier, or Aalto or their later versions of Rudolph and Kahn. It is evident that most architects will line up on the other side from Ruhnau. Hence I can classify him here as "eccentric."

Other eccentricities are of a more modest character—at once less effective and less attractive. They have, not surprisingly, been most common in churches. Defensible in terms of the technical problem are the strange tetrahedral gable windows Konrad Sage provided for the Epiphanien-Kirche in Berlin, 1960. The problem was to provide a new entrance, altar, and light for a partly damaged church of 1906; the solution is so aggressively contemporary that it does fall in the eccentric category. It is hard to understand even the rationale
4 for the same architect's church in Neu-Westend, also in Berlin. All I can see is a masochistic search for discrete ugliness in every component, a quest which was largely successful, as it has been in the United States at Stamford and elsewhere. A similarly strange result has been obtained by Fehling and Gogel in their concrete churches in Berlin-Schöneberg, the St. Norbert's church, and the
140 Paul Gerhardt church. The tower of this latter is spectacularly bad, the rest just unnecessary and purposelessly brutal. The worst of all is the church St. Ansgar in Hansaviertel, by Willy
5 Kreuer.

However, an example of the fact that brutality

[7] *Architekt Werner Ruhnau und seine Konzeption, ibid.* Translation.

4
Berlin-Charlottenburg.
Kirche Neu-Westend.
Konrad Sage, Karl Hebecker

5
Berlin-Hansaviertel.
St. Ansgar.
Willy Kreuer

and directness are not in themselves necessarily ugly or self-defeating in churches is offered by Helmut Striffler's two churches in Mannheim, the Evangelische Trinitätiskirche, to be described later, and the Evangelical church at Blumenau, just out of town. The latter is a tiny church for a poor congregation and the architect felt he had to create a sense of space inside a small volume. This is his rationale for the wedge shape and the roof which rises sharply toward the altar. Despite the obvious reminiscences of Le Corbusier, we may classify this building as having its own originality and as an example of successful eccentricity. Can the same be said of Aalto's church in Wolfsburg or of Schädel's grim Regina Martyrium in Berlin? An interesting example which might be classed as eccentric is Egon Eiermann's Matthäus-Kirche in Pforzheim. Later the reader may wish to compare this with the similar treatment of Beton-Glas in the same architect's larger Kaiser-Wilhelm-Gedächtniskirche in Berlin. Whether this trend toward brutalism, as the German architects find it possible to use more concrete, is devoutly to be wished, I do not know; but that it will come to Germany as it has to Japan is I think certain. What is not so certain is that "the readiness is all." Perhaps Germany will be spared the worst excesses by rapid shift of fashion.

As I reflected on what may be going to happen in Germany, I realized how much narrower the range there is than here. Though one can find modest examples of rough concrete, or romantic brickwork, of decorative (or nondecorative) screens, of structuralism, of bland precast modules, in short, of almost everything we see here, the examples are seldom as extreme, as good or as bad, as can be seen in America as one ranges down from the mannered Rudolph, the earthy Breuer and Sert, through the skillful, modest compositors such as TAC is and SOM has been, the suave

elegance of Johnson, the mystic romanticism, perhaps medievalism, of Kahn, the Finno-Japanese romanticism of Belluschi, the polished sobriety of Pei, the imaginativeness of Weese, Rapson, and Soleri—all these on the up side; and then down through some big names who always try for robust forms and have a positive talent for getting them wrong, down further to the screen-makers, and then down to the bottom of the big architectural operators from California who make too much of the face of our country. It is then one realizes that the spread of architecture in Germany is far narrower. This at once makes architectural life in America more exciting and more confusing. It means we will produce things more horrible than any conceived in Germany and things more wonderful. I have no doubt in the end we can be legitimately chauvinistic about this. Though our over-all scene is not a handsome one, we need not spend much time listening to an Englishman declaiming about the mess that is man-made America save as it is leveled at our countryside where our performance is definitely inferior not only to that of England but to most of Western Europe. But on architectural terms the only important good examples to be found in England are more than a hundred years old. France and Italy offer a number of more recent examples, and Scandinavia still more; but the final reflection on eccentricity or its absence in Germany leads to the conclusion that ours is a fine country for architects and a fine country in which to watch the changing architectural scene, even if every so often our architects, like the horn player, blow in so sweet and hear it come out so sour.

6
Mannheim. Evangelical
Church at Mannheim-
Blumenau.
Helmut Striffler

7
Wolfsburg.
Heilig-Geist-Kirche.
Alvar Aalto

8
Pforzheim. Matthäus Kirche.
Egon Eiermann

15

Wiederaufbau

There has never been a time when noble architecture has been spared by war. But as war has become more total, so has the destruction. It is impossible now, and it was hard in 1943, to preserve the fiction of the open city. What could be generally castigated in 1914 when the "Huns" destroyed Ypres and Louvain was generally accepted as inevitable a quarter-century later. The "atrocity" of Coventry was repeated many times in Germany with two differences: The Fortresses by day and the Lancasters by night did a more thorough job than the Heinkels and the Stukas ever achieved, and in the process they destroyed architectural monuments of considerably greater importance than that of St. Michael's in Coventry. A few places such as Heidelberg were deliberately removed from the target list; edifices in the country such as the baroque churches at Wies or Banz, nonindustrial villages such as Dinkelsbühl, were hit only by accident. But in a war of strategic bombing, few cities can really be excluded as targets. Once a city became a target, none of our bombsights was accurate enough to spare individually important buildings had it been our disposition. But even if we had had the accuracy and the desire to save them from the bombs, the "fire storms" that followed were capable of no such discrimination. In the circumstances a great many historic German buildings were razed or badly marred.

It has not been uncommon to dismiss this as unimportant on the ground that German architecture was generally second rate. It was sometimes conceded to be picturesque, but in a Black-Forest cuckoo-clock sense, a beery architecture clad in lederhosen, reminiscent of Rumpelstiltskin, Mad Ludwig, or Baron Ochs. If taken more seriously, it would be called late and derivative, marred moreover by German tendencies towards sentimentality, pomposity, and vulgarity. All this was in

9
Speyer. Cathedral.

10
Ulm. Cathedral.

some degree true. But it would be about as fair to say that British architecture is overly smug and cozy, French architecture overly cerebral and cold, and Italian architecture overly exuberant. There is nothing in Germany more vulgar, for example, than the popular Blenheim Palace.

The facts are quite different from these stereotypes, impressed by too many French and British historians and critics. Until 1944 Germany abounded in distinguished historical monuments, flavored, of course, by German conditions and German taste. There were fine remnants of Rome on the Rhine and Moselle, though not as elegant as those in nearer Provence. The Rhenish Romanesque was noteworthy for its fine arcades, its great double apses, its aspiring and multiple towers, its monumental apsides and roofs. The brick version 9 of North Germany was unique.

German Gothic religious architecture certainly lacked the majesty of the English, the brilliant structure, the aspiring naves, and the rich iconography of the French; but the "hall" churches were something special, and there have been no towers 10 superior to those of Freiburg and Ulm. The best known, the cathedral in Cologne, *is* derivative, late, long a-building, and quite atypical. One should think rather of Freiburg, Limburg, Ratisbon, and Ulm.

German secular Gothic was among the best, second only to that of the Low Countries. There were many notable German town halls in such cities as Brunswick, Münster, Lübeck,[8] built in a time when there were no better painters in the world than Dürer, Cranach, and Holbein.

The great house tradition carried on into the Renaissance. The German palaces of the eighteenth century, such as the Zwinger in Dresden, Charlottenburg and Bellevue in Berlin, Benrath 11 in Düsseldorf, or Ludwigsburg near Stuttgart,

[8] Also Hildesheim, Cologne, Ratisbon, Ulm.

19

12
Nymphenburg. Castle.

11
Ludwigsburg. Castle.

13
Brunswick. Half-timbered house behind the Church of St. Magni.

14
Vierzehnheiligenkirche.
Balthasar Neumann

were perhaps feeble copies of the great French and Italian designs, though not inferior to the British. But the baroque gardens of Ludwigsburg, the Herrenhausen gardens of Hanover, and the whole array of buildings at the Nymphenburg outside of Munich certainly had and still have great elegance and charm. Then there were the princely plans of such places as Karlsruhe and Wiesbaden and the finest of all the German secular baroque buildings, Balthasar Neumann's Residenz in Würzburg for the prince-bishop Schönbron.

The Germans in this time were making other important architectural contributions too. They built beautiful farmhouses in the Black Forest and in Bavaria. They produced great arrays of woodwork in their sixteenth- and seventeenth-century patrician houses, created the splendid step gables, the ornate guild houses, the later town halls, and other public buildings. Many of these had, no doubt, sentimental and picturesque overtones, at least for those who were not Teutons. To them must be added the magnificent and romantic but not sentimental outpouring of the baroque in the eighteenth-century churches and monasteries, from Neumann's Vierzehnheiligen to Dominikus Zimmerman's Wiesenkirche. There is no more exuberant, charming, and tasteful baroque or rococo anywhere, and we should remember this rather than that the German eighteenth century culminated in the Brandenburger Tor (1788–1791). Every country has had its unhappy "triumphal" gates.

German nineteenth-century architecture was generally a caricature of what was bad enough in other countries of Europe. In the early twentieth century, however, Germany furnished most of the architectural innovators. There were none from England after Sir Joseph Paxton, and only Pier Luigi Nervi from Italy. The Scandinavians, the Swiss, and the Germans were the great leaders, while the French supplied Auguste Perret and the towering Le Corbusier. America has only Frank Lloyd Wright whom the Germans admired more than he admired them.

The architectural revolution began in Germany very early, perhaps when the Grand Duke Ernst Ludwig established his Künstlerkolonie on the Mathildenhöhe in Darmstadt in 1899, with its atelier and five dwelling houses, an anticipation of the Bauhaus. This, despite the later acrimonious split with the Jugendstil, opened an epoch. The leaders at Darmstadt were Joseph Maria Olbrich and Peter Behrens, the latter the teacher of Walter Gropius, Ludwig Mies van der Rohe, and Le Corbusier. Later there was the Bauhaus which, under Gropius, was no doubt one of the two greatest forces moving the development of twentieth-century contemporary architecture, the other being, of course, the theory and practice of Le Corbusier.

Naturally, then, Germany boasted many tangible monuments of this revolution. Berlin abounded in them.[9] It was with little doubt the architectural capital of the world during this time as it had never been before; and, beyond Berlin, Stuttgart was renowned for the Weissenhofsiedlung, Hamburg for Fritz Höger's Chilehaus, Hanover for the Anzeiger Hochhaus on the Steintor, also by Höger. Only Munich and the picturesque towns lagged behind. Hitler and the Nazis put an end to all such ideas of design, but they did not burn the buildings. That was left for us in the process of ending Hitler.

[9] A list in unavoidable. It would include Peter Behren's Turbinenfabrik (1909); the schools of Max Taut; the Siedlung Britz (1925) of Martin Wagner and Bruno and Max Taut; houses of the twenties by Richard Neutra, Erik Mendelsohn, Hans Poelzig; Bruno Taut's and Hugo Häring's Siedlung Onkel-Toms-Hütte of the late twenties to which many others contributed, including Alexander Klein and Hans Poelzig; the Luckhardts' row houses, also of the twenties; Mies' Lemke House of 1932; Bruno Taut's art-nouveau house in Neukölln of 1910, and Max Taut's office skyscraper in Kreuzburg of 1932 with its open glazed stair wall which is still a popular and handsome feature of German buildings; Otto Bartning's clinics of the early thirties; Emil Fahrenkamp's polished Shell House of 1931; Max Taut's and Franz Hoffmann's advanced office building for the Allgemeiner Deutscher Gewerkschaftsbund of 1922; Hans Poelzig's converted Grosses Schauspielhaus (1920), later called Friedrich-Palast; the classic works by Peter Behrens for the AEG between 1909 and 1912; Mendelsohn's buildings on the Lehniner Platz for WOGA, AG of the mid-twenties; the Grosssiedlung Siemensstadt of 1929–1931 with work by Hans Scharoun, Otto Bartning, Hugo Häring, and Gropius; Hans Hertlein's factories for Siemens; and along with this, the quite different work of Fritz Höger such as the church on the Hohenzollernplatz or the earlier Scherk-Fabrik.

15
Berlin. Turbine works.
Peter Behrens

16
Berlin. Britz housing
development.
*Bruno and Max Taut,
Martin Wagner*

17
Berlin-Wilmersdorf.
Church at
Hohenzollernplatz.
Fritz Höger

18
Berlin. Grosses
Schauspielhaus.
Hans Poelzig

When you survey the rubble of your loved and familiar history, stretching from third-century Gaul to the day before yesterday, with the task of rebuilding a city for today and tomorrow, you have a wide theoretical range of choice. Shall you tear down all the broken and calcined walls that remain and start out to make a complete and brave new world? Shall you do the best you can to restore completely all of the damaged or even razed buildings, good and bad, useful and useless, seeking somehow to return to the world of day before yesterday? Shall you try to restore completely only a few of the more noteworthy buildings, using some agreed-on if loose definition of noteworthiness? If some of the ruins were of noteworthy buildings but beyond repair, shall you keep any of them as mute memorials in the spirit of St. Michael's Coventry, for example? In the remaining demolition, where you are neither going to restore as faithfully as possible nor preserve ruined shrines, shall you rebuild at least some areas "in the spirit of the old" without trying for a meticulous repetition of the ancient details? Shall you forget the spirit of the old altogether and build as well as you can for the present; and finally, if you build in the contemporary vernacular but near to ancient undamaged or skillfully restored monuments, shall you ignore them or try to be polite to them?

Save for the mutually exclusive choices of a total restoration or a totally new city, the rebuilders of each German city elected to combine a number of these alternatives. They set out to make faithful restorations of some of the most ancient, loved, and perhaps distinguished buildings on their old sites and usually for their old purposes; they elected to leave some of the ruins as memorials; they tried to rebuild some quarters to function in the manner of the old quarters and to create comparable impressions and amenities, the most difficult of the tasks and the least often successful; they sought to rebuild some areas in quite new ways and even for new purposes; in the new building, they were sometimes tender and neighborly to the adjacent old, sometimes aloof and rude.

With the possible exception of memorials, these are about the choices that have to be made in American redevelopment, at least in old cities. Restoration abroad corresponds here to preservation of individual buildings or quarters. The solution of trying to work in the spirit of the old may be a good one when it involves preservations of scale, intimacy, privacy, freedom from the automobile, and thus some of the preservable values of the old town. We have not often tried this sort of restoration but have actually achieved it in a few instances, for example, in Philadelphia. This is something we might do better with more rehabilitation and fewer demolition programs. But solutions to the same questions may lead to visual imitations and to synthetic communities, at best like Williamsburg or Santa Barbara, which are not much superior to Disneyland but only express a different taste. Most of the German efforts to recreate the spirit of the old seemed to me to be failures—only modestly picturesque at best, likely to become less convincing with every passing year and soon to be as quaint and phony as the tourist trap of "Petite France" in Strasbourg when compared, for example, with Aigues Mortes or Mont St. Michel, with Lüneburg or Dinkelsbühl, or indeed even with the tourist-conscious Carcassonne and Rothenburg. The area around the Rathaus in Stuttgart, forming a new market square, the comparable quarter of Düsseldorf, the region of the Römer in Frankfurt, some of Freiburg, all of these are, I am afraid, failures except for the buildings which were fully and faithfully restored. The restored Böttcherstrasse and Roselius House area in Bremen, which

19
Frankfurt. The Römer Area.
View after reconstruction.

20
Münster. Restored arcade
near marketplace.

was one of the most synthetic even before it was damaged, all in the spirit of the Alice Foote Mac-Dougall restaurants of my youth, might have been rebuilt more successfully in a less quaint modern way. The only exception I would care to note might be at Münster, and this principally because the great arcaded medieval streets such as one can still see unspoiled in some parts of Bern continue to contribute a great deal to modern life, particularly in shopping areas where they shield the pedestrian from the weather and the automobile while letting him be out of doors. The new arcades of Münster are pleasant to use; and if at times there is the unnecessarily romantic effect of duplicating a medieval step or construction or some other defect, it can be forgiven. But the rest of the efforts of this sort were, I am afraid, not well done and perhaps incapable of being well done; and if this is what Ernesto Rogers meant when he called the Frankfurt restoration "a phenomenon of a merely culturalistic nature," and generalized that "the truth of an old environment cannot be repeated and the new requirements have not been expressed," then he was no doubt completely right.

But there is one important principle which the new arcades of Münster, for example, reveal. If arcades were useful for urban life in 1939, they may still be useful in 1964, whether they are legacies from classic Rome or medieval Germany or eighteenth-century France. It is the principle of the arcade that should be examined, not its ancient pictorial quality. If pursued in this way, a city can maintain much of its past without any false sentimentality. Thus if one can see quite clearly in Frankfurt what not to do, he can also see what might have been done. And one should scrutinize Santa Barbara or the Avenue of the Americas quite as critically as Frankfurt.

The question is much simpler, or so it seems to me, when it comes to whether one should restore an old building which had great distinction or sentimental value. A list of the precise restorations in the new German cities would show a preponderance of cathedrals, town halls, or large burgher houses which can be turned to useful official purposes, or palaces which are now to be museums. The old cathedrals are fully as marvelous places of worship as the shining new churches—indeed, one can only say this with tongue in cheek for it is a gross understatement. No one who has not become a dogmatic ideologue can regret the restoration or repair of many of the great old churches in almost every city.[10]

The German Rathaus is in many respects ceremonial; much of the bureaucratic town business can be done in other quarters. The old Rathäuser and their attendant Ratskellers had marvelous qualities which are still virtuous, and such buildings perform as well as a new job by Kunio Mayekawa or Kallman, McKinnell, and Knowles, perhaps better. One can only applaud the decision to restore the distinguished ones like the Rathaus of Bremen, the great Rathaushalle there and the Rathauskeller on which Heinrich Heine lavished so much affection.[11] Where they were less distinguished, as at Mannheim or Düsseldorf, doubts arise and in such cases one tends to prefer Stuttgart's new one even though its modernity is along romantic, eclectic lines.

There have, of course, been some restorations other than those of cathedrals and town halls. The

[10] For example, St. Petri in Bremen, Sankt Aposteln and the Cathedral of St. Peter in Cologne, St. Bartholomeo and St. Nicholas in Frankfurt, the cathedral quarter at Freiburg, the Marktkirche in Hanover, the Marienkirche, including the Totentanz windows, in Lübeck, the cathedral at Münster, and so on.

[11] Or the Römer of Frankfurt and its fine Kaisersaal although this is not historically correct with respect to its original medieval appearance, the Kaufhaus in Freiburg, the old Rathaus of Hanover, the magnificant Stadtweinhaus Münster.

21
Hanover. Marktkirche.
Dieter Oesterlen

22
Frankfurt. Rathaus.
Imperial Chamber.

23
Münster. State Wine House
after reconstruction.

24
Stuttgart. New Rathaus.
Paul Stohrer,
Hans Paul Schmohl

City of West Berlin, for example, has enacted a law for the preservation of monuments which would include restoration where necessary. The approved list includes 141 items—parks, palaces, hunting seats, manor houses, town and village churches (ten out of the thirteen village churches were heavily damaged; nine have now been repaired), and individual monuments that span history right into the twentieth century, including works of Taut, Wagner, Bartning, Gropius, Scharoun, Behrens, Poelzig, and Fahrenkamp. Such a program will appeal to the historically minded in America. If one were applied here, Pennsylvania Station, New York, and the Robie House in Chicago would perhaps be preserved. But perhaps not. Each of the Berlin buildings can more or less continue to serve a living function although it also happens that they are landmarks of architectural history, some major, some minor. The question might run this way. First, should you preserve anything you would not think worth rebuilding had it been destroyed? To this I rather think the answer should be "no." And if you are to preserve or rebuild, should you do either unless there is a clearly useful, almost pragmatic, present purpose for the building? Here again I think that the answer should be "no," unless the building is an outstanding piece of architecture on some absolute scale, or has played an outstanding historic role (Independence Hall). A city cannot become a museum of architectural history, much as some historians and sentimentalists would like to have it so. On such terms, it is right that Pennsylvania Station should not have been saved, although one might have hoped for a more significant replacement.

In Chicago, the Robie House is one of the better domestic works of perhaps our greatest American architect. It is not near to the total interest offered, for example, by the house of Jacques Coeur in Bourges; it does not suggest the architectural invention made earlier by Wright in Unity Temple. It is not a document characteristic of life in Chicago at a given moment in time, as, for example, any number of seventeenth-century New England houses are for their communities. But atypical as it may be, made by an atypical architect for an all-too-typical client, it is no doubt at least as important a landmark in American time as, say, old Fort Duquesne. There may be nothing better of Wright's to preserve from this period; but even if there were and the cause were not a national one, there might be local justifications. On somewhat similar terms, excepting the fame of their architects, it is perhaps right, though I am afraid marginal, that Berlin should preserve and rebuild the Charlottenburg Palace or Schloss Bellevue since there are better examples of the style and period elsewhere in Germany (but not very accessible to Berlin). We could accept them as marginal, but if we are to be that critical then we must concede that AEG Moabit and Shell House must also go when changing technology writes their utility down to too low a figure, just as Wright's Larkin Building had to go in Buffalo. Good housing is more durable. For example, the housing of the Fuggerei built by one of the Fuggers in Augsburg in 1520 is still viable housing and even better than that.

Perhaps as historical monuments the restoration of the Dürerhaus in Nuremberg and the Goethehaus in Frankfurt are marginally acceptable, although the Kilroy effect must always be watched in such installations and even a great man is a Kilroy on some of his visits. What shall we say, for example, of the Beethovenhaus in Bonn or the "Buddenbrooks" House in Lübeck? What is one to say, further, of the Laveshaus in Hanover or the opera house there, a common example of the kind of opera houses fashionable when the Paris Opera House set the pace? It was a classic revival building of 1845–1852 designed by a well-known

25 far left
Hanover. Laves House.
Georg Laves

26 left
Hanover. Opera House.
Georg Laves

27
Hanover. Burgstrasse,
reconstructed.

Hanoverian architect of the day, Georg Ludwig Laves, and was so much admired by the Hanoverians that with the help of large public donations it was restored and reopened before Christmas 1950, a remarkable achievement.

As we will see later, there are some excellent new opera houses and theaters in Germany, but the total experience they offer is not always as rewarding as an evening, say, in the restored and totally charming little baroque hall built by François Cuvilliés le Vieux in 1751–1753 in the Residenz of Munich, scene of the first performance of *Idomeneo* long, long ago. The Hanover Opera House is no Cuvilliés theater, but it may serve the Hanoverian operagoers quite as well as a new one would have done.

One can, I think, become a little less tentative about the new Burgstrasse in Hanover which provides a convincing impression of being an old street. It has been reproduced with genuinely old houses brought from various parts of the destroyed city so that this Burgstrasse might actually have existed, although in fact it never did. The deception is no greater to be sure than that of Monticello or Mount Vernon or any other historic American house that has been equipped with furniture authentic to the period although never actually used by Jefferson or Washington. If to this is added the cleaned-up effect in our colonial monuments provided by ladies who prefer order to truth, a strange view may be gained of what Monticello was for Jefferson. In view of the range of Jefferson's interest, the suspicion lurks that during his residence there Monticello may have looked more like Oyster Bay than it is now permitted to. But if one pursued such logic to the end, the streets of Williamsburg should be knee-deep in ooze and the nonarchitectural details of Hanover's Burgstrasse should be in keeping with the time of the buildings whether or not this would be acceptable to modern

standards of convenience and sanitation. At what level, in other words, does the lie of restoration become intolerable? The Burgstrasse is charming to look at. Everyone will have to consult his own judgement as to whether it is too much like Spenser's Duessa to be admired. The thornier question of what it might mean to one who did not know the original had best be left unasked. Are the great cathedrals of the Ile de France only lies since the ministrations of Viollet-le-Duc? Where *is* the line to be drawn?

But the Burgstrasse does illustrate another problem of restoration or preservation, which is whether the restoration or preservation of single buildings is in fact satisfactory, or whether one must always think in terms of "quarters." It would be ridiculous to claim that the vast Cathedral of Cologne does not fit well into its present new environment, indeed dominate it. The great cathedrals of the Ile de France, since Viollet-le-Duc set out to make them more visible, do not fail to impress and please, regardless of the fact that their present environs are not a fair representation of those in the Middle Ages. Indeed, the hemming in of the West Front of Bourges is today an annoyance, and not only to photographers. Perhaps the answer is on a sliding scale: The more distinguished and impressive the building, the less important may be its historical ambiance, but if the buildings move toward modest anonymity, as is true for every building on Louisburg Square, Beacon Hill, Boston, the flavor of the quarter becomes more important.

The German reconstruction of the great marketplace of Bremen has allowed for new buildings without destroying the integrity of the old. The Rathaus and perhaps even the Roland statue before it are good enough so that they could have been allowed to stand in an otherwise modern square. But they are clearly enhanced by the restoration of

31

29
Bremen. Schütting, main
square.

28
Bremen. Rathaus.

30
Bremen. Savings Bank,
main square.

all the other buildings on the square. This is, however, not a purist restoration. The Haus der Bürgerschaft, for example, will be visible, and it is contemporary. The Schütting, the old guildhouse of the merchants opposite the Rathaus, which has a sixteenth-century façade with many changes of 1896, is not like the Rathaus at all but helps the square nonetheless. Even the transfer of the rococo façade of the Pflügerschehaus, which faced the Schlachte before the bombing, to the new Sparkassenhaus on the Markt seems to me on this occasion justified. The Bremen square is charming now, and it is going to be a pleasant though historically untruthful place when, according to plan, it is freed of all automobiles.

Perhaps the same acclaim can be granted with a little less conviction to the squares in Lübeck and Münster, maybe even to the cathedral area of Freiburg, but only if the automobiles are banned. It cannot be awarded to old Nuremberg, which is depressing now if one knew it before; to Munich, which continues to preserve its part-baroque, part-nineteenth-century, part-Bavarian-farmer quality and brooks little else; or to the squares of Stuttgart, Brunswick, and least of all Frankfurt.

Even the good restorations may no longer be meccas except for tourists. A modern Bremener who lives out in the Neue Vahr, may have little reason to come to Bremen center often. He will not care to go to church in the cathedral, or will have no business to transact at the Rathaus or with the various organizations which will occupy the restored guild houses; he may not find a meal in the Ratskeller good enough to warrant the trip, especially if he has been used to the big ornate wine barrels, long empty. He may not be led to feel as warm toward the market square as Heine felt when he wrote "Happy the man who is safe in the harbour, leaving behind him the storm and the sea, and, at long last, now sits warm and peaceful in the

friendly surroundings of Bremen's Ratskeller." It is perfectly possible that the market square of Bremen and the adjacent Böttcherstrasse may in the end be of little value to people of Bremen save for the tourist marks they attract; and if this should turn out to be so, then it may not have been worthwhile to have done the restoration at all.

Finally, one has to ask if the restorations have been well done. On the whole, a superficial observation uncoupled to deep concern about the historical record would yield a favorable response. I am not disposed to attempt any detailed assessment. The most interesting of the jobs to me was Dieter Oesterlen's Gothic Marktkirche in Hanover, dating from the fourteenth century. Except for its strong tower, this was a very simple church with brick piers, walls, and vaults. It was hard to get proper brick and even harder to find masons who could rebuild the piers and especially the vaults. For the latter, many were tried and only a handful chosen. Yet the rebuilding was accomplished and it will, with one exception, be hard to tell the rebuilt church from an old one, once time has modified color and texture. The exception is that there was no effort to reproduce the original doors. Instead, Oesterlen commissioned Professor Gerhard Marcks to design some new bronze doors "in the spirit of our times," relying in part for source materials on old Gothic gravestones. The details of the doors, like those on the doors designed by Ewald Mataré for the Cologne cathedral, are far from abstract and hence would no doubt be repudiated by many contemporary sculptors and critics. They have indeed a close kinship to the archaic details of the leaves of San Zeno Maggiore in Verona or those of Sankt-Michaelis-Kirche in Hildesheim. They do not hesitate to refer explicitly to ancient symbols (the pelican), to Old Testament stories (Jonah), to events of the Works and Days (ploughing), or to local history (the burning of Cologne). Thus they resemble in spirit the iconography and the sculptural treatment of the Romanesque days. Yet they are among the most effective applications of sculpture to architecture made during the era of rebuilding.

When the Germans had to build new buildings alongside of old and more or less prized ones, they encountered the same difficulty which confronts our contemporary architects. No one can seriously contemplate slavishly following the old details in the new buildings. They are both inappropriate and impossible to have well executed. But more serious is the problem of the new material, the new use, the new scale. A special problem is raised by memorial situations, and I will discuss it separately. But most situations are not memorial situations; and in them I found that the German architects have run the same gamut, plumbed the same depths, and as seldom scaled the heights as American architects, but with somewhat more solicitude, it seems to me, for the old; perhaps there is more agreement that the old does deserve some respect. However, the whole range of possibilities is demonstrated somewhere or other in Germany.

Hanover offers three examples, each quite different and in its own way successful enough, although collectively a little unhappy. There is first of all the pair of essentially contemporary 31 buildings located very near the Rathaus. The Rathaus itself is a grand monster of Victorian (or Hohenzollern) style, complete with gigantic cupola erected in 1901–1913, which, perhaps unfortunately, escaped much damage. Its rear has a splendid lookout over the arbored Masch Lake and like so many buildings of the era it had fine large spaces, often very ornate, monumental stairs and foyers, and a grand room at the rear also enjoying the lake vista. Since much of it was left standing and the large rooms were useful, it was almost inevitable that it would not be razed despite its lack of history. The Hanoverians put it back into shape with *brio* and with no false penury. The outside they patched up as need be; the inside they redecorated with modern-style furniture, fixtures, and other decor, expending no effort in emulating what was thought to be opulence in 1900. Even the great entrance doors of the formal meeting chamber of the City Council were executed in contemporary terms in iron-nickel alloy by the Hildesheim goldsmith, Blume. The effects are pleasant, if a little grandiose, and it does not seem especially ironic that the old-fashioned foyer should house four very large models of Hanover as it was in two periods before the bombing, as it was in 1945, and as it is envisioned for the future.

Another lesson of the Hanover Rathaus might be heeded, for example, by Harvard University which has shown so much hesitation about what to do with its Memorial Hall since a fire destroyed its tower. Memorial Hall was a rather frightening landmark of Victorian Gothic, but a landmark nevertheless. Like the Rathaus in Hanover, it was not without a certain majesty. Like the Rathaus, it was not so badly burned that demolition was obvious. Harvard had two strong choices. One was to tear Memorial Hall down and build a new and more timely replacement; the other was to restore the building *including the tower* without worrying unnecessarily about the expense. The university chose neither of these alternatives but instead the weak compromise of simply patching the roof to keep out the wet and using the place as best might be until something else happened. The Hanoverian conclusion was more positive. The lesson does not apply only to Harvard. I can remember other examples, such as the face-lifting proposal to save the historic old post office in St. Louis which resulted neither in a good new building nor a real reminiscence of the old.

But this is not the whole story of the Rathaus. 32 Next door is the new Kestner Museum, a kind of memorial piece, enclosed in a contemporary cocoon. Near at hand are the two much larger buildings which serve as offices for the building administration, replacing rather fully destroyed older buildings. These are frankly contemporary. The lower building of four stories is of frame and panel construction, its skin mostly glass. The 33 higher one is different in its fenestration, but its ends have a curious screen which has no particular harmony with the walls of the Kestner or the Rathaus. The two elements are connected by a still lower all-glass high-ceilinged loggia the main entrance to which displays a monumental piece of old stone bearing the Hanoverian lion and unicorn. As described, this combination of Rathaus, museum, and new buildings for a bureau certainly sounds chaotic. It did not seem so at the time of viewing, but on reflection this may have been because, as an outsider, I was incapable of becoming indignant at the "desecration of Hanover," or because the Rathaus is after all so much more imposing than the new buildings that they are only pinpricks, or

31
Hanover. Rathaus.

32
Hanover. New Kestner Museum.
Building director, Werner Dierschke

33
Hanover. Department of Public Works, Administration Building
Building director, Werner Dierschke

because of the many trees. Perhaps it helped to build the background for the uneasy feeling I had when leaving Hanover that although it is a cultivated city, and although Dieter Oesterlen is a sensitive architect and human being, and although Rudolf Hillebrecht enjoys the highest of reputations as a German city planner, Hanover has not yet become the pleasant place it must have been in the nineteenth century.

Another Hanoverian example to be paused at more briefly is the Wangenheim Palace. This 1829 building, also by architect Laves, was destroyed during the bombing. It has been restored to supply offices for the Ministry of Economics and Commerce (Wirtschaft und Verkehr) of the State of Lower Saxony. But more space was needed, and this was provided by a new and contemporary building of no great sensitivity which has little compatibility with the Wangenheim except that of size. Due to the difference between Renaissance fenestration and modern glass panel walls, even the scales are not compatible. In this case as well as in the Rathaus group, the new buildings manage to make the old designs seem better.

The Wangenheim Palace is on the other side of the street at a diagonal from the Rathaus and Kestner Museum. It forms one end of what is to be a plaza lined with state buildings, and opposite it will be the old Leineschloss. The reconstruction of the Leineschloss is at once the most dramatic and successful of the Hanoverian efforts to marry the old and the new.

34a The Leineschloss was a far more distinguished building than the Rathaus or the Wangenheim Palace. It was first built in 1637–1640 by Duke Georg and was extensively rebuilt from time to time, including substantial changes by Laves between 1817 and 1842. But it was never completed, so the monumental Corinthian portico never stood on the central axis but at one end. It was so fully gutted by the bombing that only the walls, the window frames, and the portico remained standing. 34b When the decision was made to rebuild and enlarge it to house the parliament of Lower Saxony, there was a competition as is usual on such occasions in Germany; this was won by Oesterlen. His design retains the Corinthian portico as the main entrance and much of the detail of the southeast wing but puts the portico much 34c more nearly on axis by a massive plenary hall wing. The side wall of this wing is made of large panels of granite facing that are suspended in front of concrete walls, alternating with steel graphite colored windows. The base courses are of the same sandstone as the palace. Three enormous standard-bearers of bronze project from the plain granite wall of the main façade: sculptures of sun, gale, and rain-wind by Professor Jürgen Weber. The contrast between the two parts of the façade is firm, even assertive, in everything except scale and color. 34d Inside, the rooms are all modern in spirit, especially the excellent inner courtyard with its glazed corridors. It is a successful marriage in which each partner goes its own way with due respect for the other; and, granted the decision to keep anything of the old palace, the solution was no doubt about as successful as could have been expected. Certainly a purer solution would have been obtained by demolition—but whether better is harder to say, although the completely new Parliament Building 154 of Baden-Württemberg in a park in Stuttgart suggests this might have been so. European architectural history, though, is full of successful combinations of this sort (for example, Hampton Court Palace); and whether these will in the end be the contributors to cities that are more satisfactory for human beings than the dictated unities of Chandigarh or Brasília or the bulldozed ones of American urban redevelopment remains to be known.

What the main ingredients of happy coexistence

34a
Portico before bombing

34b
View after bombing

34c
View after rebuilding

34d
Interior, showing foyer

34
Hanover. Government
headquarters of Lower
Saxony: Leinschloss.
*Architect of new wing,
Dieter Oesterlen*

35
Düsseldorf. Mannesmann
skyscraper.
Schneider-Esleben, Knothe

36
Cologne-Ehrenfeld. St.
Anna's.
*Gottfried and Dominikus
Böhm*

40

are must be clear to any competent architect. They involve first of all scale, including the scale of windows and other details, proportions, and to a lesser extent rhythms, textures, and colors. These are central. Compatibility is quite impossible at the urban level if a gargantua shatters the urban scale as Pan American does in New York and Prudential in Boston and these could not succeed even if their details were better than they are—they demand an entirely new scale of the city. It is modesty in these attitudes which has preserved central Paris and to a considerable extent rebuilt Germany, more than the "politeness" of the newcomers which is no greater in Germany than here. It is not "politeness" then that matters. It is something more sensitive than good manners. A few years ago most modern architects ignored the problem of compatibility. Now most of them pay lip service to an ideal which their actions do not support. But possibly if they talk about it long enough good action may follow. This is not at all a matter of resisting change, only a matter of finding a way to change gracefully.

We may run swiftly over a few other German 35 examples. In Düsseldorf there is a new glass-and-metal tower built as an addition to the solid office block of the Mannesmann steel corporation designed years ago by Peter Behrens. The detail has been done with great care by Paul Schneider-Esleben and Herbert Knothe, and the building has a high reputation. Only an ideologue and theorist would want to maintain that the Behrens job and the Schneider-Esleben designs were visually more compatible than the Hanoverian examples previously cited. Yet the arrangement is less disturbing and this is, I expect, because each is really an excellent exemplar of the style of its time. To my taste, the Behrens part is both handsomer and more useful than the shiny new tower, but then I am perhaps more tired of unmitigated glass than I ought to be.

Such problems often arise with churches and seem to be easier of resolution. Belluschi, for example, came off better with his Church of the Redeemer in Baltimore than he has with additions to secular buildings and neighborhoods. One of the most successful of our contemporary architects in showing a sensitivity to the old was the late Eero Saarinen. He showed it, I think (saving the eagle), in Grosvenor Square, and less controversially in Ezra Stiles College at Yale and the new Law School Library at the University of Chicago. In both these latter and more successful accommodations, the preceding architecture, though secular in purpose, was ecclesiastical in form. In Cologne the new chapel in Sankt Aposteln offers no affront to the old Romanesque apse. An even more interesting example is the very modern church, which the 36 Böhms built for St. Anna's in Cologne-Ehrenfeld where all that was left standing was a Romanesque tower. The success is all the more noteworthy since Dominikus and Gottfried Böhm, who often designed with much Romanesque reminiscence when they were making new churches, evidently felt no such impulse when working in the shadow of genuine Romanesque remains.

But there are bad examples, too. One can be too practical and abrupt, as one observes at the Hotel am Zoo at the foot of the Kurfürstendam in Berlin. Originally the well-known dwelling house of Alfred Messel, it was converted into a comfortable, even luxurious, small hotel in 1911. It was rebuilt and enlarged in 1950 and 1957 by Paul Baumgarten, who is usually a good architect. At the Hotel am Zoo, however, he added two new stories, slightly set back but in highly conventional contemporary style. The outside is ugly. The upper stories inside, furnished as might be expected by Knoll International, are really not as luxurious as the older, larger upholstered rooms with the enormous bathtubs still to be found, thank the

Lord, in many parts of Europe. In the interests of modern design, we are gradually reaching back to the low standards of comfort acceptable in the Middle Ages. It is time we remembered that the Victorians were not immoral because they wished to be comfortable, that beauty is not synonymous with austerity and discomfort, though it is better that the uncomfortable contemporary be handsome, as in the Hotel am Zoo, than vulgar, as in the Berlin Hilton.

The outstanding examples of bad juxtaposition are in Frankfurt. The worst is to be found in the environs of the medieval Eschenheimer Turm impinged on by such not-very-good contemporaries as The Bayer and the Telecommunication buildings. The Eschenheimer tower is naturally much the best looking and at the same time the least useful of the buildings in the immediate vicinity. But it is stifled in a way that the Roman ruins are not, even in Trier; it is less compatible with its present than Chicago's frivolous old water tower on the near North Side; it is an impediment to traffic and I suppose it would be more sensible to tear it down or move it somewhere else since it is daydreaming to imagine the same delightful prospect for the Bayer and the Telecommunications.

Perhaps one gets a new perspective on the problem of the old and the new when one goes to a country about which he has not accumulated sentiments, so I have somewhat revised my views on politeness and impoliteness since my visit to Germany. I am not certain that to seek an obvious visual compatibility will result only in disaster, though literal matching as proposed for the Houses of Paliament in London, will be. I am certain that when the old buildings have a certain simplicity, such as that possessed by the Romanesque or the American colonial versions of Georgian, a sensitive person can do well, as TAC did for example at Andover (I saw nothing as skillful as this juxta-

position in all Germany). When the old architecture is complicated, as in the Gothic or the baroque, the problems get harder and can probably be solved only by contrast. If the old is not only complicated but also not very good, as was true of most Victorian work everywhere, the problem may become impossible to solve. You had better go ahead then and do the best you can including demolition. But doing your best is the crux, and this means worrying about the old things for a while, approaching them with sympathy even if you cannot approach them with affection or reverence. If you are good enough, as Le Corbusier was at Harvard, perhaps you can just forget anything else is there, but I am not sure. If you are not that good and try to shout down the old just to prove how wonderful you are, then the bad things will be born. I think there has been very little of this exhibitionism in the German efforts and if often they have failed, it is on an absolute rather than a relative scale. Of course, if both the old and the new are first class, maybe compatibility is no issue. But do you really believe that the Taj Mahal and the Parthenon would look well on opposite ends of the same garden? That is the question. Otherwise, we must accept the fact that cities will change even when they have not been bombed and that time and habituation are great remedies for architectural failures. But they are ameliorants, not cures, and some mistakes may even seem worse with time. This will be equally true, I think, of the nostalgic German efforts to lug in souvenirs of their past work as integral parts of new designs and of such unidentified and even artificial reminiscences as displayed in the Huntington Hartford Museum in New York or the Perpetual Savings and Loan Association Building in Los Angeles. I guess if that is the choice, the Corinthian portico of the Leineschloss is more fun and more transparently "honest."

Denkmäler

Most peoples have built memorials to the ordinary dead, to the illustrious dead, to heroes and more rarely to poets, to what seemed at the time to have been important events, thus to be remembered for a long time, to victory, or to defeat. We have samples of all these kinds in our own country except to our defeats, which we have never admitted. We did not, for example, preserve the burned White House of 1814 as a permanent reminder of the "savagery" of Englishmen. The Germans have, however, been notably interested in memorials and the postwar reconstruction has carried with it a new superabundance. But there are some differences in spirit from those of other years.

Almost no victory symbols were possible. There are two exceptions. One is the Russian tank which rests in a little Russian enclave in West Berlin, just a few yards from the Brandenburger Tor, an extraordinary and ironic reminder. The other is indeed a memorial to a kind of German and Western victory. It stands at Templehof and is an abstract but perfectly explicit sculpture by Eduard Ludwig commemorating the success of the Air Lift.

Fortunately for everyone, the savage advice given by Allen W. Dulles on May 11, 1946, went unheeded: "Berlin, like Carthage, has represented the spirit of destructive conquest. It has lost its right to be the capital of the Germany of the future. . . . The city is without a real history, without landscape, without architecture and without charm." In the heat of the moment this pious and democratic man as many a pious man before him then went on to propose exactly what a Nazi might have proposed for different reasons for Lidice, that the inner city should be preserved in its state of ruin as a "perpetual memorial to the Nazis and to Prussia."[12]

Nonetheless, though for more complex reasons,

[12] Allen W. Dulles, *Collier's* Vol. 117, No. 19 (May 11, 1946), pp. 80–81.

38
Berlin-Tempelhof. Memorial
to the Air Lift.
Eduard Ludwig

the Germans have themselves preserved ruins of the bombing. There is something like this in almost every city. It is usually the hulk of a church. Sometimes, as in Darmstadt, it is nothing but the silent ruin. This is essentially the case for the Nikolai Chapel in Hanover of which only the choir remains standing. Another example also in Hanover is the Aegidien Church.

More often something has been added to the ruin in the form of a small devotional chapel. Characteristic of the idea but particularly notable in the execution is the Sankt Kolumba Chapel built by Gottfried Böhm in 1950 in the ruins of the late Gothic parish church in the Brückenstrasse, Cologne. It is a simple octagonal space, with a flat tent roof supported by thin concrete ribs. One enters it from the darkness of the old tower and meets a sculpture, St. Anthony blessing the fishes, by Ewald Mataré, and windows by Ludwig Gies filled with an angel choir in blue and yellow. Other art includes windows by Jan Thorn-Prikker and Georg Meistermann, and the "Trümmer-Madonna," a late-fifteenth-century sculpture that was saved from the old church.

The most famous of these arrangements, partly no doubt because of its location and partly because of its size (some, but not I, might say because of its distinction), is the Kaiser-Wilhelm-Gedächtniskirche built by Egon Eiermann in 1960–1961. It is located on Breitscheideplatz at the foot of the Kurfürstendamm, where no visitor to Berlin can miss it: The location is even more pivotal than that of the Arc de Triomphe in Paris. The original building, a Romanesque revival affair erected between 1891 and 1895, was not very old, not very distinguished; but it was the church of the Hohenzollerns many of whose portraits still hang undamaged in a small portion of the unruined hall dedicated to the memory of the first Emperor Wilhelm. Around this hulk and its damaged tower

39
Berlin. Kaiser-Wilhelm-Gedächtniskirche.
Egon Eiermann

Eiermann has erected a platform. From the platform spring a large octagon and a tower, both of steel skeleton filled in with elements containing glass that create a blue light. The light is reflected both inside the octagon, which serves for devotion, and outside the tower, which looms blue against the street at night. The complex was the winner of a competition; Eiermann is one of Germany's most highly regarded postwar architects; the location is spectacular. But for all that, I found the Kaiser-Wilhelm-Gedächtniskirche neither meaningful, nor moving, nor beautiful. For us it may say, "be careful what you seek to remember."

Three other unusual examples are to be found 40 in Münster, Hanover, and Cologne. In Münster, Harald Deilmann incorporated a piece of the wall of the old theater in his new and fine ultramodern one. Here as visitors walk the foyers during intermissions they can cast a reflective glance at a not very noble ruin. A still more curious case is that of 41 the Kestner Museum in Hanover. The collections of this museum, spared by the war, were distinguished. The eclectic building which housed them was not. Its back wing was destroyed by the bombs, and there was other damage. The old space had in any event become inadequate. The solution of Werner Dierschke, made in 1959–1960, was to wrap the old affair in a larger building whose honeycombed façades enclosed more area and threw good light on the objects shown in the peripheral rooms; the old rooms were retained in the old shell which in itself then became a museum piece. The new museum is good, but it would have been still better had the old core been demolished, for the sad truth is that the old building, whatever its merits as a conversation piece, was simply not good enough to be so embalmed alongside of distinguished examples of ancient Egyptian and Etruscan art and fine minor objects of the Middle Ages.

The most successful example of this sort of enterprise, and I suspect the most durable, is the 42a Gürzenich in Cologne, restored and enlarged by Karl Band and Rudolf Schwarz. The first Gürzenich was begun by the city in 1441 as a place to receive guests of note. The first festival was held in 1475 to celebrate the visit of the Emperor Frederick III. Similar celebrations occurred throughout the years up to the eighteenth century when it began to be neglected and finally fell in ruins. It was repaired in 1855 and then served not only for official parties of the city but for some kinds of exhibitions, concerts, meetings, and for carnivals. Housing also a popular restaurant, it became an important downtown civic resource. It was severely damaged by the bombs. Even more heavily damaged was the adjacent old loved St. Alban's Church, which lost everything but its external walls. The new St. Alban's, designed in modern terms, was built on a far removed site, and ruins of the old were incorporated into the new banquet hall.

Back in 1931, Käthe Kollwitz had created her over-life-size sculptures of the "Mourning Parents" to stand in the Belgian military cemetery at Dixmude where her son, a soldier of World War I, was buried. Ewald Mataré, a Rhenish artist, returned from exile in 1945, made a replica to be placed in the ruins of old St. Alban's as a memorial to the 50,000 people of Cologne who lost their lives in World War II. Apart from Käthe Kollwitz's own personal grief, these sculptures seem to have a very special meaning to Cologne and her people. Yet they also embody parental grief anywhere and 42b thus a stranger may be moved by them. They can be seen from the street, but that is not all. For as Band and Schwarz repaired the old Gürzenich and added a new section joining it to the St. Alban's ruin, they saw to it that the great stairs and balconies of the stylish and gay foyer offered views

40
Münster. State Theater.
Foyer, showing section
from old theater.
Harald Deilmann

41
Hanover. New Kestner
Museum. Foyer, showing
old museum façade.
*Building director,
Werner Dierschke*

42
Cologne. Gürzenich.
Rudolf Schwarz, Karl Band

Above
Gürzenich façade

Right
Gürzenich. View from
foyer window of ruins of
St. Alban's.

through windows down onto the broken floor of St. Alban's and the kneeling, mourning old people. It is a seemly juxtaposition of joy and sorrow, a reminder that life is in fact a mixture of both, and a quite direct, rather Greek statement of the comic-tragic paradox.

One cannot be confronted so frequently with these memorial ruins without wondering what they are all about now and what they will all be about a half century hence whether they are in Cologne or Coventry. You can read them a number of ways. The German ones are not exactly reminders of "Furore Teutonico diruta: Dono Americano restituta," the inscription which Whitney Warren unhappily designed on instructions from Cardinal Mercier for the library rebuilt at Louvain after the First World War, or the same thing as Allan Dulles urged in his unfortunate *Collier's* article of 1946. But there is, of course, something of that in them; and I have no doubt that a good deal of the early German thinking about them was directed to the notion that they should constantly recall the horror and absurdity of war and genocide and perhaps also offer some prayerful admonition not to be led that way again. Thus there may be, at present, in the German view of these memorials combined feelings of nostalgia, of reaction against war in general, and of guilt or remorse. But all of these may be hard to sustain over time. The nostalgia will not exist for oncoming people who never knew their city when these buildings were whole, and it can hardly be revived for them if it is clear that the buildings were not all that good anyway. The sight of bombed ruins can probably not provoke a reaction against war in the minds of those who never have experienced a bombing, or who know without experience that these little souvenirs give no inkling of what a modern war would be like with radiation lurking in the ruins. Finally, a nation cannot be made to feel guilty over

generations and there may be something pathological in asking unborn youth to contemplate symbols of parental remorse—and even risky for these ruins can quite as easily be construed by a demagogue as incitements to revenge as reminders to regret.

This is equally clear, it seems to me, of the somewhat smaller number of explicit references to Nazi tyranny and murder, aimed at the present internal situation. How long, for example, will there be a lesson in such a monument to victims of Nazi persecution, erected in Hamburg by Heinz Jurgen Ruschewegh? The most recent of these is the Catholic church, Regina Martyrium, erected in Berlin in memory of the Jewish victims of the Nazis. The building, by Hans Schädel, is brutal; the abstract bronze sculpture of the fourteen stations of the cross by Herbert Hajek even more brutal; the tower is overpowering; and the mural behind the altar, by Georg Meistermann, reminiscent of a weak imitation of Bolotowsky, is uncharacteristic and unfitting. I found it quite impossible to feel any of the appropriate sentiments here. They come much more easily when viewing the modest revival in Berlin by Jews themselves. Here on the Fasanenstrasse, just across the street from the Hotel Kempinski, stands the new Jewish community center on the site of the Hessel Synagogue destroyed in 1938. The new building, by Knoblauch and Heise, incorporates the portal of the original synagogue and a memorial column, but it is designed mainly as a center for Jewish life in Berlin and a meeting place for both Jews and non-Jews. It is these functions that do for the sentiments what the more obvious effort at Regina Martyrium does not. It is achieved on the Fasanenstrasse with no dramatic assist from architecture. None of Germany's remorseful memorials has the sheer power of reminder of the Fosse Ardeatine in Rome, for the Fosse could be concrete about individuals, with names, while the reminders of Nazi murders involve abstract millions. Yet as time goes on I come more and more to question whether abstract expressions of remorse are a good idea. Paintings like "Guernica," great poetry, or other writing (which, curiously, has not emerged), sculpture which would do for the weeping parents what Michelangelo did in the unfinished Rondanini "Pieta"—all these outpourings of the human spirit might create a permanent record. But it is very hard for architecture or architectural ruins to say so much. Convincing statements on subjects of this sort are more likely to come from the spontaneous outpourings of artists than from carefully planned official regrets, no matter how sincere. With the exception of the Gürzenich which contains a transcendental suggestion, I suspect these remnants are a bad idea, and just as bad whether in Darmstadt or in Coventry. But you will find a lot more of them in Germany. They really are a characteristic of the Wiederaufbau, and an unfortunate one, I happen to think.

But so, come to think of it, are most modern architectural memorials. It may be true as Erwin Panofsky says that there has been no important tomb sculpture since 1700. It seems clear that Monticello is a better reminder of Jefferson than the classic memorial on the Potomac or the wishbone which is rising on the waterfront of St. Louis. For one Lincoln Memorial or Cenotaph or Invalides there are hundreds of Grant's Tombs and too many Mount Rushmores. It is a sobering thought. The Victorians liked memorials and apparently liked what they got whether it was in verse or in brick. We *think* we like memorials and do not like what we get or even what, like the Franklin D. Roosevelt Memorial, we do not get. We seem unable to separate the personal involvement and taste of a presidential family from the national need. People and events are not long remembered

through the naming of streets or the lighting of eternal flames, or the erection of sculptures and architecture. Even Bacon's effective memorial to Lincoln in Washington owes least to its architecture, more to its statue of Lincoln, and most of all to Lincoln's words inscribed in the wall. Great architecture will never arise for small purposes; and if we are not getting good memorial architecture it is perhaps because we do not, in the long run, look upon architectural memorials as important.

43
Berlin-Charlottenburg.
Maria Regina Martyrium.
Hans Schadel,
Friedrich Ebert

The Arts and Architecture

The Germans seem to have tried harder than American architects to join the arts to architecture in so far as finding budgets for art pieces is concerned. But the difficulties often go beyond budgets. There are, in the first place, not many good artists; among the good ones, not many of the talents are architectonic; the architects have not offered the artists very good areas in which to work. You cannot, for example, expect Albers, Kepes, and Lippold to do well in spaces such as those in the Pan American Building, where the architecture interferes with any good vantage point from which to see the art. Finally, and unlike the great architectural art of other times, there seems very little for the art to say. I do not know how any sculptor could be expected, for example, to make a statement about the U.S. Plywood Company which would justify sculpture in that company's new building on Third Avenue, New York, on anything more than merely decorative grounds; and the difficulty is compounded when it turns out that the building is not the creation of the company but that of an entrepreneur. How do you go about expressing such entrepreneurs in art, unless you are Goya or Daumier?

It is not really much easier when one is dealing with public buildings. Would it be possible to express the United States Department of State and American foreign policy in our embassies, now that the eagle is happily out of fashion as a symbol if not as a policy; and if it were possible, would it be desirable? More might be done with the Peace Corps, but buildings are not their main concern.

The church remains the principal bastion of the architectural arts, as indeed it always has been. In America, many denominations seem to have become ashamed of symbols or at least of any which can be understood. This has been less so in Germany, so heavily Catholic or Lutheran, and German church art has been helped as well by a greater freedom from the fear of being archaic, derivative, eclectic, and from the stylish and almost universally held notion that it is better in the arts to make a poor innovation than to do well in extension or restatement of an already established tradition. So German liturgical art may be, at its best, more effective than American, but unhappily it is not often at its best.

Of the various arts, it is true in Germany as it has been here that sculptors have come off best. Again, the German sculptors, like the architects, have no doubt profited from living in the midst of an excellent local history extending over a longer period and provided with a richer outpouring than has been the American experience.

There are still such things to be seen as the second-century relief of the Celtic goddess Epona; the touching Romanesque carvings of the cathedral at Worms, where such works as the Christ King in the tympanum of the old south portal or the half-relief of Daniel among the lions, both of about 1200, are the peers of any of the French Romanesque sculptures; the gilded bust of Reinhold von Dassel, Archbishop and Chancellor of Barbarossa, created in 1220 for the Shrine of the Three Kings in the Cathedral of Cologne; the Romanesque door leaves of Sankt Maria im Kapitol of 1000–1030 with their scenes from the life of Christ; sixteenth-century work such as that of Heinrich Brabender in the Cathedral of Münster; Gothic market wells like the one in Brunswick; the later fountains which began to bring in secular subjects, both regal and peasant, including the fountain of Henry the Lion in Brunswick, the city lion of the same city, and the famous fountains of Nuremberg; the gilded tympanum of Freiburg Cathedral, the Baroque "Fourteen Holy Helpers" of Vierzehnheiligen, the fifteenth-century carvings of Tilman Riemenschneider; and from our own times, the earthy sculpture of Ernest Barlach (d. 1938) and Käthe Kollwitz (d. 1945). As in the case of architecture, you will not find many citations of German sculpture in American, British, and French critical works; but this only partly results from judgments of its inferior quality, and these are not always correct. There was a good enough tradition, and German artists were aware of it, whether or not anyone else was.

Indeed, some of the best of the recent German architectural sculpture has been made by men who were well aware that they were in the footsteps of Barlach, whose "Totenmal," executed in 1927, is still to be found floating above the slab to the war dead of 1914–1918 and 1939–1945 in the Antoniterkirche in Cologne or of Käthe Kollwitz, whose "Trauernde," copied by Ewald Mataré, stands as already mentioned, in the ruins of St. Alban's, Cologne.

Of the successors, two men have perhaps done the best. Gerhard Marcks was already working in this vein in 1930–1932, and in 1947 some of his sculpture along with that of Barlach was placed in the façade niches of the St. Katharinenkirche in Lübeck. In his more recent work he was commissioned by Dieter Oesterlen to make the doors for the restored Marktkirche in Hanover. This is an altogether effective metal door, in quite modern form though representational, and in Romanesque spirit, too, if a little more archaic than the work of Marcks' predecessors. It does not hesitate to make references to ancient symbols from the old iconography, to Old Testament tales, and to old-fashioned peasant activities, so that the subject matter is thoroughly familiar (as it should be); yet neither the arrangements nor the details are in any way copied from the Romanesque despite, for instance, the characteristic emaciation of the Christ. Thus this sculpture is a far greater contribution to the architecture than has generally been achieved by the abstract sculptors. Of course, the architecture itself is archaic.

At his best, Mataré has scored similar successes. His archaism is a little more evident. He uses the symbols of the Middle Ages with more familiarity and has combined them with reminiscences of the burning of the city as on the previously mentioned new south doors of Cologne Cathedral. The relationship of the separate elements is less com-

44
Cologne. St. Anthony's.
Sculpture: "Totenmal."
Ernest Barlach

45
Hanover. Marktkirche.
Door design.
Gerhard Marcks

46
Cologne. Cathedral.
Bronze relief on south door:
"Burning of Cologne."
Ewald Mataré

47
Cologne. Cathedral.
Bronze relief on south door:
"St. Ursula."
Ewald Mataré

pact and less explicit than the panels, say, of San Zeno Maggiore or for that matter of the old leaves of Sankt Maria im Kapitol, and there is a not altogether happy intrusion of more than one metal; but these are, nonetheless, good contemporary ecclesiastical art, serving their purposes well. To deny this would require that one be determined to accept no art of our day that is conceived in this spirit. I do not know why any one should let critical demagogues shame him into that absurd and inflexible posture. Mataré scored a somewhat comparable success in his St. Ursula, also on the south portal, installed in 1948. These works are in no great conflict with the older sculpture in the niches of the same portals which were spared by the bombs. He has been less successful when he has tried to construct his own archaism as in the prophesying angel on the gable of the bishop's seat at the cathedral of Essen. The angelic lady (she certainly seems feminine) with her beaded raiment and her suave wings is somehow overly reminiscent of the wax angels which turn up in perfumers' windows the week before Christmas. Lioba Munz's hanging crucifix of enamel and gems in the new St. Alban's Church of Cologne is of the same archaic, even barbaric, character but more reminiscent of Byzantine ikons than of Romanesque sculpture. Still more primitive and fairly effective is Denis Boniver's attenuated and moving crucifix in the Neue Paulus-Kirche in Essen-Altstadt-Ost, installed in 1958–1959.

Another well-known sculptor, Hans Mettel, has done well with contemporary primitivism in such works as the deliberately crude St. Bartholomew relief in the cloister of the cathedral of Frankfurt-am-Main or his suspended cross in the Maria-Hilf-Kirche, Frankfurt. He has been less successful with his incised designs, such as the Christ in the Matthäus-Kirche or the Madonna flanked by six figures which is cut into the brick

48
Cologne. St. Alban's.
Hanging crucifix.
Lioba Munz

49
Frankfurt.
Allerheiligenkirche. Incised
figures.
Hans Mettel

50
Frankfurt.
Allerheiligenkirche.
Tabernacle of the Last
Supper.
Albert Welker

51
Cologne. St. Theresia's.
Silver-chased sculpture:
"Baptism of Christ."
Hans Rheindorf

52
Hanover. Georgsplatz.
Sculpture: "The Breeze."
Aristide Maillol

53
Hanover–Calenberger
Neustadt. Sculpture:
"Child in the Rain."
Kurt Lehmann

54
Hanover.
Hoffmann-von-Fallersleben
School. Sculpture: "The
Seesaw."
Ewald Brandt

49 façade of the Allerheiligenkirche, also in Frankfurt. The relative poverty of the idea is manifest when one thinks of the treatment of similar subjects in Romanesque and Gothic days. Albert Welker's
50 Tabernacle of the Last Supper in the same church is more effective. That primitivism or archaic eclecticism is no guarantee of success is evident in many other efforts in Germany, such as Günter Haese's reliefs on the north wall of St. Anna's in Düren or the conventionalized apostles flanking the altar of the Herz Jesu in Neunkirchen, and most sharply in such stronger works as the silver-chased baptism of Christ by Hans Rheindorf in St.
51 Theresia's, Cologne. This contemporary primitive realism has in a few instances proved as distinguished as any recent German architectural sculpture, but its successes have not been sufficient to establish a principle.

It has, however, been more successful than other types of representational sculpture. There are some distinguished pieces such as the marvelous
52 Maillol on the Georgsplatz in Hanover or work by Henry Moore at the Academy of Fine Arts in Berlin or in the Planten un Blomen, Hamburg; but these works are neither German nor directly applied to architecture. Of less modern quality but still attractive, reminiscent, and an addition to the streetscape is the literal goose fountain on a wall in Düsseldorf.

Mostly, though, these efforts are weak, as is the Mutter Gottes, which Kurt Zimmermann carved out of marble for St. Joseph's Church in Cologne or the Fischerbrunnen in front of St.-Lambertus-Kirche, Düsseldorf. Often they are simply "cute,"
53 such as Kurt Lehmann's "Child in the Rain" in Hanover. There are many pieces of sculpture of this sort in housing projects and even more in schools, whether as literal as those of Kurt Lehmann, or Hermann Scheuernstuhl's sweet group on the Aula of the Leibnizschule, Hanover.

Kurt Schwerdtfeger's "Children's Round Dance" in the Volksschule Grimsehlweg is slightly more
54 abstract, and Ewald Brandt's "Seesaw" in the Hoffman-von-Fallersleben School is amusing and well-composed. All of these examples are from Hanover, but comparable things can be found in most parts of Germany. The general situation is discouraging if one believes that children learn to appreciate art by being surrounded by it. One wonders what it is that they are learning to appreciate. Of course, none of the work of this sort approaches the inane mediocrity of "The Berlin Bear" by Renée Sintenis, marking the entrance to the beleaguered city where the autobahn reaches Zehlendorf, or the "Phoenix" at the entrance of the Bundestag in Bonn. It is regretful because a great deal of effort has gone into procuring sculpture for public places, and most of it is quite representational, unconvincing, and not really better than Disney, though duller since less vulgar.

Unhappily for theorists, efforts at greater abstractions still derived from obvious and literal sources have not usually been any more successful. Aside from the Moores and from Le Corbusier's well-known and highly personal reliefs at the Berlin Unité d'Habitation, the most effective piece
55 is no doubt the Jerusalem altar by Klaus Arnold in Oesterlen's Martenskirche in Hanover. Another
56 of the few good ones is Maria Becke-Rausch's "Conversation" in the inner court of Hanover's Leisure House. A pleasant example of play sculp-
57 ture is O. Baum's the "Lochofant," of dark gray poured concrete in the yard of the Silcher elementary school at Stuttgart-Zuffenhausen. It is too bad more children cannot experience such things instead of depressing abstract humans such as Bernhard Heiliger's sculptures at the Ludwig Georg School in Darmstadt, which stand starkly in a very stark play yard. Heiliger can do better as he showed in the cast-aluminum

55
Hanover. St. Martin's.
Altar screen. Relief showing
the 12 gates of Jerusalem.
Klaus Arnold
56
Hanover-Linden. Recreation
Center. Sculpture:
"Conversation."
Maria Becke-Rausch

abstraction he made for the main entrance of the German pavilion at Brussels. Children meet unimaginative work outside the schools as well. There are such things as Fritz König's granite cows in a housing project in Munich (real cows would have been better), or Kurt Zimmerman's bronze couple in front of the German Red Cross in Bonn, or the dreary pair who stand on the lawn of the Beethovenhalle, also in Bonn. The latter are almost funny, but probably not to German children who take their art seriously.

It would be convenient but wrong to conclude that these are failures (and mostly they are failures) because the sculptors were on the wrong track in pursuing any kind of representation. This is probably not the reason; rather, they unhappily do not have the talents of a Maillol, or a Lachaise, or a Moore (neither do ours). The weakness of the ideological explanation appears when one looks at the efforts to produce abstract symbolism along new lines.

I saw only one piece of this sort that seemed to have real if modest quality. This was Eduard Ludwig's three-pronged memorial to the Airlift erected at Templehof in 1951, a fairly explicit statement about an important event. Sometimes these efforts are simply not very convincing, as in Herman Schand's doors for the Rathaus in Essen, which are already beginning to slide to the *kitsch* and the commercial. The strictly commercial ones may be fairly acceptable, such as the panels of the apothecary's garden in Hamburg's Planten un Blomen, or even the obvious sign for the insignia of the International Show of Ladies' Wear at Düsseldorf, but ideas like this are meretricious to start with and tend to degenerate as rapidly in Germany as they do on Madison Avenue. We need no bad examples to add to our own performances in this field, but we could find them easily enough in Germany.

There then remains the work of the pure abstractionists. There is some of this in Germany, too, no more convincing and no less so than that of their peers over here. There is Hans Uhlmann, who likes to hang rods as he did with some success in the entrance hall of the library at the University of Freiburg, or to bend plates into a sort of stabile as he did with less success in front of the Berlin Opera House. Less success? To be utterly candid one would have to say that the Opera House would be better off without it.

A more interesting use of abstraction is to be found in the bronze doors by Helmut Lander for Oesterlen's Christus-Kirche in Bochum, where the material was poured into molds manipulated in advance to provide patina and a design which is an abstract statement of the passage from Exodus:

Da sprach der Herr zu Moses:
Siehe Ich will Euch Brot vom Himmel regnen
lassen. (*Exodus* XVI:4)

The most famous of the abstract sculptors is no doubt Norbert Kricke, who generally but not always bends tubes. He has received the full accolade of such a distinguished and sensitive critic as Carola Giedion-Welcker and certainly has taste, skill, and a sense of proportion. Pieces such as the "Grosse Kasseler" with its delicately balanced equilibrium and some of his other spatial sculptures are very interesting, even beautiful. But I am less convinced of the architectonic qualities of this work. Thus the applications to the Stadttheater, Münster, and the larger and more recent application to the Theater-Studio in Gelsenkirchen do not seem to transcend decoration and may not be good decoration. The curved piece designed to go on the plaza between the Mannesmann Building and the river in Düsseldorf is a special case. Seen by itself, it has considerable

58
Bochum. Christ Church.
Bronze door.
Helmut Lander

59
Spatial sculpture:
"Grosse Kasseler."
Norbert Kricke

quality. Seen against the building, its relative scale is not right. It is not Kricke's fault that most of the time it is seen with its top rising from a sea of parked cars and that then it simply looks ridiculous.

In sum, the architectural sculpture of Germany is abundant and not very good. Except for some of the archaic work like that of Marcks and Mataré at one end and the abstractions of Lander and Kricke at the other, the Germans are not doing anything we are not doing as well or better. This is discouraging because we are not doing very well very often. It is discouraging because we should be buying art profusely for our schools and colleges and public places. And it should be contemporary art. But there is no sense (in fact it is stupid) in placing bad art in public places. There may not be enough good sculptors to go around, just as there are not enough good architects. Single examples such as the work by Antoine Pevsner, "Construction in Space in the Third and Fourth Dimension," at the University of Chicago Law School continue to offer hope.

60a
Düsseldorf. Mannesmann skyscraper. Spatial sculpture.
Norbert Kricke

60b
Same Mannesmann setting with cars.

65

62 right
Cologne-Mülheim.
Notkirche.
Otto Bartning

63 below left
Düren. Christ Church.
Helmut Hentrich,
Hans Heuser

64 below right
Frankfurt. St. Wendel's.
Design for south window.
Georg Meistermann

61
Berlin-Charlottenburg.
Church at Lietzensee.
Paul Baumgarten

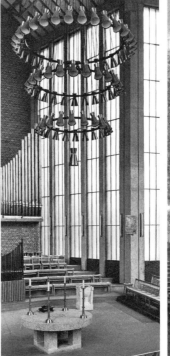

Unhappily, with the exception of some glass designs, even worse things must be said of the other arts. There is no general current convention as to how to use glass in churches in Germany just as there is none here. It seemed to me, however, that the range of ideas is wider there between using windows simply as lightgivers and on the other extreme as more-or-less literal statements of a conventional iconography. In a great many of the churches, the windows are of ordinary uncolored glass supported in a variety of frames, and intended either to bring light into every part of the church or to throw light into a particular area. There is a fine expansive window offering a view of the woods outdoors behind the altar of Paul 61 Baumgarten's church at Lietzensee in Berlin. The glass may be used as a clerestory encircling the 62 altar as in Otto Bartning's Luther-Notkirche in Cologne-Mülheim. It appears in a most interesting form in Helmut Hentrich and Hans Heuser's 63 Christ Church in Düren. Here the plan is that of a Greek cross with the sides tapering from the center to the ends. The ends are plain brick, the eight tapered sides essentially all glass to make a church that is very light, yet full of shifting contrasts. Rudolf Schwarz was fond of high horizontal lighting: He provided it almost all the way around St. Michael's in Frankfurt; in company with vertical slot windows at the Liebfrauenkirche 129 in Cologne-Mülheim; and in a larger size on one entire side of the nave at St. Anna's in Düren. As is fairly common in the United States, large windows on one side only are used to light the altar at Alois Giefer and Hermann Mäckler's "Maria Hilf" in Frankfurt or to light an important 75 mural, such as Georg Meistermann's in back of the altar in St. Alfons', Würzburg. Meistermann has created an unusual big south window in St. 64 Wendel's, Frankfurt, which is mostly of plain glass but has two or three carefully placed pieces of color and message.

When the German window designer started to come bearing messages, even in churches, he seems to have encountered the same difficulties that bothered the sculptors, such as what messages, what symbols, and so on; and very often he has given up and retreated into the pure abstraction of color à la most of the windows in Belluschi's American churches or, for that matter, the higher standards set long ago by Auguste Perret in his church at Raincy, which only the work of Kepes outdoes. But the window designers seem also to have been more reluctant than the sculptors to rely on historical stimuli either in symbols or in techniques. It would be hard, if not impossible, to create medieval tracery today; and even if one could, the delicacy would be quite out of place among the crudities of the architectural designs which are always present in contemporary churches, sometimes with deliberately powerful effects, sometimes just as a confession of the total clumsiness of many contemporary building crafts. But even if the tracery were available and appropriate, the glass does not exist nor does the affection for miniatures, whether created by the assemblage of glass pieces or by painting. Thus it is hard to imagine any contemporary glass painter or glass assembler being ready or able to depict twenty scenes from the life of Christ or the life of a saint, from the stories of Lazarus, or the Prodigal Son, or the Good Samaritan, the Golden Legend, the Resurrection, or any other of the subjects which were dealt with so richly in Bourges, Chartres, Amiens, and Beauvais, or to work such wonderful *grisaille* as that of York Minster. When they have tried, as Emile Frey did in St. Louis, results have seemed tepid. Moreover, the vigor of the old messages has given way in Catholicism to the softness of Marianism and in the Protestant churches to doubts about atonement through substitute and thence to social welfare and mild ethics, which are hard to portray in modern terms and which were not the most dramatic sources even in the Middle Ages as Good Samaritan windows and lozenges of the Virtues and the Vices will attest. In these circumstances it is not surprising that the window makers have not been very successful; and if the sculptors seem to me to have been more effective, it may be because my own aesthetic heart is still in the highlands of the Middle Ages so that I overrate the sculpture which looks backward while discounting the glass which is certainly *not* looking backward, if indeed it is looking anywhere.

The simplest of the symbolisms and the most literal even if quasi-abstract is to be found often in the depiction of anonymous angel choirs such as Ludwig Gies provided in the St. Kolumba Chapel, Cologne. The colors are simple and thin, yellow and blue with some neutral glass. The angels' heads are mere circles, and their raiment and wings fall away in cascades of triangles and related forms in an effect which is somehow reminiscent, though not richly, of Duchamps' "Nude Descending a Staircase." The same reminiscence is even more marked, with tear symbols and Picasso-like forms thrown in, in Georg Meistermann's choir window in St. Kilian, Schweinfurt. The effect is certainly pleasant and mildly religious, but I would not expect any contemporary to be "sent" by the simple notion of angel choirs. The symbolism seems trivial, and the distance between the art and a Christmas card is not great. (Not that good Christmas cards are undesirable but just that they should not be major elements of church design.)

The literal symbolism of angels turns up in other forms, too, simpler and even less desirable as in the memorial chapel on the ground floor of the tower of the Maria Königin Church by Dominikus Böhm in Cologne-Marienburg. The space itself is very strong with its heavy stone and brick work, its huge marble slab, and the poignant fifteenth-century crucifix hanging above the altar. In a black and white photo the abstract angels which occupy windows on three sides seem quite in scale at least with the architecture. But another scale to consider is that between the architecture and the crucifix. The scale of the windows and the scale of the crucifix are not compatible because the angels' oval heads are so much more monumental than the head of the Christ. Moreover, the color is too strong. As sheer abstractions of the heads and wings of angels these windows are no doubt more convincing than the windows by Gies in St. Kolumba, but they are not really appropriate where they are; and as in the other case, I wonder how much is gained by the contemplation of an egg which, thanks to the wings, can be interpreted as the head of an anonymous angel.

In other areas, Maria Königin is more sophisticated, if perhaps a little overly intellectual. It is described as the "tent of the Lord." The principal effect of the main interior is best felt on entering the square main room from the low-ceilinged confessional chapel or the baptistery. The four slender columns that support the roof do suggest tent poles, especially as the roof is arched. The west wall curves concavely behind the altar, which though not central remains the focus, seeming to stand amid the congregation. The effect is much enhanced by the large window of seven panels which fills most of the south wall and may suggest the linkage of nature with the Holy Sacrament, though on thoroughly non-Thomistic terms. Indeed, one can see through the glass to the pines here and there. As planned by the architect Dominikus Böhm with the help of H. Bienefeld, the living trees are augmented by a background of tree and leaf motifs on the glass. It all cooperates most effectively with the space; and had the

66
Cologne-Marienburg.
Maria Königin.
Dominikus Böhm

65
Cologne. St. Kolumba
Chapel. Angel-choir
window.
Ludwig Gies

message-bearing stopped with this simple and important idea, this window would have been distinguished symbolically as it remains distinguished to look at. But the background motifs are cluttered up by a garland of fourteen symbols taken from the Loretto Marian litany; such symbols as the Tower of David, the Ivory Tower, the Chaplet of Roses surrounding the Crown of Mary, the Blessed Vessel, and so on require labored explanations that the nativity and resurrection symbols or the Last Judgment do not. Somehow these seem less important than the pelican, the lion, the lamb, more realistic and yet more esoteric, less familiar and yet more banal.

Another difficulty is that the messages are too prominent. As one participated in the Mass in Bourges or Chartres, accompanied by a richly composed liturgy and music, free from uninspiring sermons, one's mind was not perhaps tempted to wander; but if it did wander, it could be stimulated visually only by the complex of ribs and piers or by the rich blood-red and blue colors of the windows. That there were details on the capitals or in the windows, the familiar of course knew, but he could not make them out at long range, and so the distractions were not specific as they unhappily became in the sixteenth century when the windows told fewer stories and displayed larger figures in the telling. I would suppose the symbols at Maria Königin would be most distracting if one's mind wandered from the altar, which indeed it might be prone to do in such a light church while being treated to a modern sermon. However, the window and the big room at Maria Königin work harmoniously in a strictly architectural sense, and this underlines the fact that architectural sense is not enough. This distraction by oversized figures in a window is even greater in the chapel at Sankt Aposteln, Cologne, where the figures are positively gigantic and even menacing.

67 In another part of the Maria Königin Church, the baptistery, Böhm has designed still more abstract windows by providing two rows alternately intended to depict baptism by water and the occasional substitute therefor, baptism by desire or by blood (the martyrdom for Christ's sake of one who has not been baptized). The color effects here are rich indeed, the message extremely obscure, and the difference between trying to be convincing with such remote symbols or with more familiar material is well shown by the cover of the font in the same room, designed and executed in enamel by Hans Rheindorf. Rheindorf uses the old symbols drawn from the formularies of the Easter Saturday liturgy, all aimed at reminding the one about to be baptized of how it is in effect a symbol of the rebirth. Appropriate reminders of this are the creation, the flood, the sacrifice of the ram, the journey through the Red Sea, the prophecies of Isaiah, Baruch, and Ezekiel, the experience of Jonah, the Ark of the Covenant, the Tables of Law, and the three young men of the fiery furnace, all old and familiar. The suggestions are infinitely richer than those of the windows, which can perhaps be defended on the ground that they are but the general background statement of the specifics which are presented by the font. Yet again I felt the windows to be distracting; and the contrast between them and the font is all in favor of the latter. Much the same thing could be said for Rheindorf's tabernacle and altar cross, also in the archaic style,

68 and also not afraid of the ancient messages. It may be that I read too much into the power of the symbols themselves and not enough into the relative talents of Rheindorf and Böhm. Böhm was a considerable architect of churches, but this is no guarantee that he had much merit as a sculptor or painter. Unhappily, many architects now fancy themselves to be creative in all fields and then proceed to demonstrate that they are not.

67
Cologne-Marienburg.
Maria Königin.
Dominikus Böhm

68
Cologne-Marienburg.
Maria Königin. Tabernacle
and altar cross.
Hans Rheindorf

69
Frankfurt. Cathedral.
Window design: "The
Lord's Prayer."
Hans Leistikow

70

Mannheim. Evangelical
Trinity Church. Two views.
Helmut Striffler

There are, of course, many other examples of what I have described at Maria Königin. I am trying, though, not to make a catalogue but rather to illustrate by choice examples.

The ultimate descent into abstraction which still pretends to mean anything is the resort to writing on the glass, as Le Corbusier did at Ronchamp 69 and Hans Leistikow did when he printed the Lord's Prayer on a window of the cathedral at Frankfurt. The designs are reasonably pleasant, but it seems to me they are trivial combinations of verbal and graphic ideas in which the sole graphic contribution has become one of design. This stricture is valid even when the lettering, say, of "Marie" is in the calligraphy of the master, Le Corbusier. "Marie" gains no more power from the fact that an artist has inscribed her name than God did when Victor Hugo announced "Quant à moi, je crois en Dieu."

When the abstraction goes further, it can only go in the direction of nonmessages, which either permit the observer to let his imagination take him somewhere (as perhaps in Kepes' window in the Church of the Redeemer in Baltimore, or Mario Ciampi's abstractions at Corpus Christi Church in San Francisco), or nowhere (as in the windows of most of Belluschi's churches, Netsch's glass for the Air Force Academy Chapel, or the designs unhappily imposed on Breuer by the local artists of Collegeville, Minnesota). If you are going to encourage this vagrancy, you must not, I feel, be as strong and distracting, even if the message is unclear, as the combination of coarse steel truss forms and a huge spiral design on glass which Rudolf Schwarz and Georg Meistermann concocted at Bottrop, one of the few pieces of brutality to be found in German church design until recently.

It is better in such cases to go the familiar way of putting globs of colored glass into a concrete matrix, a natural evolution from the more formal combinations of Raincy, even if these become as gentle as Belluschi's.

This arrangement is by no means unique to Germany, but there are some good examples there. Among the best must be the strong arrangements 70 provided by Helmut Striffler in his Trinitätiskirche at Mannheim. This church is as powerful in its own way as Breuer's at Collegeville, though less fluid, and as stark though not so obtrusively so as Figini and Pollini's Church of the Madonna of the Poor in Milan. The windows flow all around the church, forming a background even for the altar and bathe the whole interior in many colors though the over-all effect remains dark, especially on the first entrance. This is a symbolic effect deliberately contrived so that later the penetrating light may perchance remind the worshiper of eternal light. Yet I wonder if this would ever occur to anyone without a guidebook. The light moreover is to be thought of as reaching the inner room not through obvious and segregated windows but through the walls themselves, which in the first encounter are conceived of as a chalice and later as a crib or manger. Here again one wonders if the fine architectural idea is obvious enough. But the whole message is not to be limited to such a simple statement as might have been made to Joseph of Arimathea by the Grail. Within the large message there are detailed messages: of chalice, crib, cross, the chalice golden, the cross violet, the wounds of Christ red. Thus from place to place purely abstract constructions in the Beton-Glas become specific symbolic reminders of such events as the Annunciation, the Incarnation, the Resurrection. The symbols are not conventional or so strongly abstracted as to be immediately decipherable. Some of them may not be decipherable at all; but they are sufficiently clear so that with time and reflection at least a few interpretations can be made

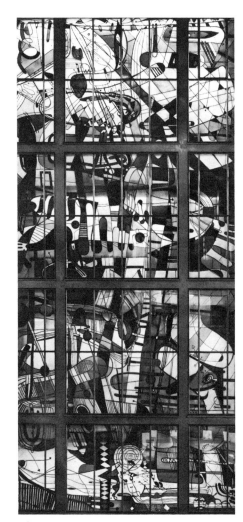

72
Cologne. West German
Broadcasting Corporation.
Staircase window.
Georg Meistermann

71
Frankfurt.
Weissfrauenkirche.
Werner W. Neumann

without help. It is a total concept and a strong one, in some senses a modern Sainte-Chapelle. As with the windows of medieval cathedrals, the worshiper can take the church as a whole or focus his thought on details, but the detail is not so large or so insistent as to destroy either attention to the Mass or private reverie.

There are many other examples of Beton-Glas in Germany, but I saw no others quite so effective. There are a few details in the Weissfrauenkirche in Frankfurt, but they are less committed than those of Mannheim, two large windows flanking the altar, various panels here and there. The regularity of the concrete network, a system of squares with various combinations of diagonals, inscribed diamonds, and other rectangular divisions, is more mechanical and less thoughtfully considered than the apparent nonpattern of Mannheim. The colors, mostly primary reds, yellows, and blues, seem to have been inserted with no greater intention than to provide a colorful pattern. Symbols when inserted are simply dumped into a panel and are explicit, such as the fish which is ubiquitous in the art details of this church. The result is above average but the concept much less aspiring than that of Mannheim and the realization much less distinguished.

Much the same must be said of the glass windows Anton Wendling provided in some parts of Rudolf Schwarz's Liebfrauenkirche at Cologne-Mülheim. Here it is Schwarz's over-all design that dominates, and the windows are distinctly subordinate in importance, and aimed mostly at providing a color note. The effect is, however, at once simpler and stronger than that of the Weissfrauenkirche.

Similar devices have been used in secular buildings with equal architectural but less suggestive results. A good example is Georg Meistermann's window-wall at the radiological institute for the University of Freiburg im Brisgau, where the concrete is much more dominant.

When glass is used for secular purposes in more conventional ways, it seems to me to have been of only modest interest even in good examples such as Ursula Hirsch's window in the stair hall of the Boniface School, Essen; or Meistermann's staircase window in the customs office at Emmerich; or his more dramatic window in the staircase of the West German Broadcasting Corporation in Cologne. The reason is twofold. First, these last examples are really paintings in spirit which happen to have been executed on glass surfaces even if the painter has chosen to break the surface with some modern geometric tracery and to take advantage of the transparency of the glass. There is nothing wrong with any of this, and it is not surprising since Meistermann, for example, is in fact a painter; but it is different and less important than the glass wall of Trinitätis in Mannheim. Perhaps there is simply more to say about the birth and the death and the resurrection than there is about a school, or the management of a customs office, or even about broadcasting.

I am convinced that the glass in Germany has been at least the equal of the sculpture and better than ours. But I am certain that as much cannot be said of architectural painting, mosaic, and other wall or floor adornments.

We might begin here with bad examples. I believe them to be typical, but one does not see everything; and even a hard-working and pretty systematic voyager may overlook some important things, or even get an over-all impression as false as Herbert Hoover had when he remarked that he had not met anyone who was going to vote Democratic.

The most gruesome of all the designs I saw was 73 the large mural provided by Helmut Lang for Gottfried Böhm's St. Theresia Church in Cologne-Mülheim, 1955–1956. This round church is pretty disastrous on many counts including Rheindorf's font which is much inferior to his tabernacle in Maria Königin. But here we must speak only of the enormous painting on an inner wall extending half the height of the church, seeming to cover the supports for a freestanding choir loft, and backed most unfortunately by a high window by Gottfried Böhm. Gottfried was never the architect his brother Dominikus was, and here he shows why most architects and especially engineers should leave painting and sculpture to somebody else. In this case, he can be censured for providing an unusually clumsy backdrop and commissioning and accepting an awkward and unconvincing painting dedicated to the life and passion of Christ. The pictures are explicit enough; the washing of the feet; the storm on the Sea of Galilee; the entry into Jerusalem; the Last Supper, and so on. Anyone could recognize them. But the drawing is incompetent; the expressions are wooden. It is not that religious painting is necessarily pleasant or beatific. Much of the greatest of El Greco or Tintoretto is

not. But there are no expressions here, no interpretations, no suggestions, simply clumsy cartoons à la the worst of WPA, and given such a denouement one can only wish there had been no art at all.

A much better painting no doubt, but quite inappropriate, is the colorful abstraction provided 74 by Georg Meistermann behind the altar at Hans Schädel's new Regina Martyrium in Berlin, already mentioned. Here the question is less one of painting skill than of meaning. I could find no relation between the purpose of the church and the purpose of this mural, or between its colorful details, almost playful, and the austerity, even brutality, of the church itself.

A more comprehensible painting, but still not 75 good enough, is the enormous mural Meistermann provided back of the altar for Hans Schädel's St. Alfons' Church in Würzburg. This is a church which is focused on the mural, and it is important that it be effective. The windows, the lighting, the convergent walls of the nave, the deep-set niche of the altar all demand attention to the point where the writer of the guidebook feels it necessary to exclaim rhetorically, "Was soll das Bild? Was bedeutet es? Was hat das mit einer Kirche zu tun?" The explanation is that the mural is in fact an altar painting, a "Gloria in excelsis Deo!"

The subject is the great and testing one of the apocalyptic vision of St. John from the famous fourth, fifth, and fourteenth chapters of Revelations: the one sitting on a throne who looked like jasper and sardonyx, the rainbow like an emerald, the twenty-four gold-crowned elders, the seven lamps of fire, the sea of glass, the four winged beasts, the book with the seven seals, the slain Lamb with seven horns and seven eyes, the predicting angels, the Son of Man with his sharp sickle, and the angels with their sickles,

73
Cologne-Mülheim.
St. Theresia's. Mural.
Helmut Lang

74
Berlin. Maria Regina
Martyrium. Altar mural.
Georg Meistermann

77

and the angel thrust his sickle into the earth, and gathered the vine of the earth, and cast it into the great winepress of the wrath of God. And the winepress was trodden without the city, and blood came out of the winepress, even unto the horse bridles, by the space of a thousand six hundred furlongs. (*Revelation* XIV:19–20)

It is an awesome and perplexing subject which has haunted religious artists since they first began to try to deal with it, fearsome as it was in the early Burgundian tympani, distilled as it became into the simple serenity of the west portal of Chartres. It is laden with esoteric visions, with symbols emerging from the depths of the Old Testament, fused with the notion of Messiah, of doomsday, of plague and war, and the Last Judgment, and in the offing the new heaven and the new earth and the holy city. It is ominous and joyful, and around it many conventions have grown. So it takes a great deal of courage for a contemporary artist to try his hand at it in quasi-literal terms; and it is hard for anyone who knows the subject well to be taxed with digging the symbols out of a composition in which sickle and beast, rainbow and throne alike seem to have been tossed with deliberate confusion. The result is less convincing than the earlier simpler and more orderly presentations; and the effect is contaminated perhaps by the overhanging angels who resemble those the Mexicans cut out of tin for festival occasions and especially for the festival of the Nativity. This is not an unimportant painting; yet though it is often possible to study for a long time such apocalyptic works as Michelangelo's Last Judgment in the Sistine Chapel or even such a minor work as that in the Cathedral of Albi, somehow one leaves the ideas of this painting quite rapidly. It is not so much that the apocalyptic vision has become old hat as that a contemporary can find so little new to say about it. Perhaps Picasso might succeed if he were to turn his mind to it, but he would not be so readily detoured by

the beatific angelic idea and would remain more concerned about Lucifer. The Apocalypse is a great and frightening test of man before he can arrive at the new world, and the fear is important. But fear is missing in this mural, in a world which should be at least as familiar with fear as were the sculptors of Vézelay, Autun, and Bourges. Still in a curious way one is glad that Meistermann made the try instead of presenting us with a few blobs of violently hued paint and a thirty-page explanatory essay of what the blobs meant and how he personally felt about the Apocalypse.

The other large example which I should perhaps mention is the mural of the Apocalypse and the Last Judgment provided by Peter Hecker for Dominikus Böhm's St. Elizabeth's Church in the hospital at Cologne. The church is one of Böhm's masterworks; the painter has been given a more generous setting, especially dramatized by the flanking tiers of arches, and he has dealt with the subject more directly, more literally, perhaps one could even say more conventionally. Though the composition is more fractured and the drawing more archaic, this painting by Hecker of 1949–1950 is more convincing than Meistermann's of about five years later. It leads to some hope that the subject need not disappear from the painter's repertoire although I can think of no one in the United States today whom I would like to see tackle it.

These are probably the best two examples of efforts to use serious painting in buildings. The secular results are generally weaker. There is, for example, if better than most, Heinz Metell's long abstract mural in the Berufsschule at Hanover. It is abstract in total effect and colorful, but it is made up of conventional symbols such as doves and fishes. This school trains bakers, confectioners, and other comparable trades. I could not help wondering what the groups would make of the

76
Cologne-Hohenlind. Church in St. Elizabeth's Hospital. Altar mural: "The Apocalypse and The Last Judgment."
Peter Hecker

77
Hanover. Technical School II.
Mural.
Heinz Metell

mural. I would not suggest that they live with the Apocalypse, either. Yet it is a good idea, I suppose, to expose them to art in their schools. Does it not matter what art? Does it not matter whether it is evocative? Bewilderment is not a good way to meet art; one can hardly expect the workers to wander around the painting with a guidebook in hand, and I wonder if it is really cricket simply to breed acceptance through familiarity.

For somewhat different reasons but mostly because it just didn't seem good enough, I was not happy about the very abstract though colorful murals Friedrich Wilhelm Kraemer had installed in his Abend-Schule and *gymnasium* near Dortmund or even those at the ends of the corridors of Dieter Oesterlen's otherwise fine Wilhelm Busch school in Hanover. Both of these buildings provide reasonable places for paintings, and the failure lies in the paintings themselves.

In general the weakness of most of the art in the German schools is disheartening. For if ever there is a time in the growth experience when the association with art should be free, natural, and healthful, it is in the school experience. On balance it probably must be said that unless good art can be commanded for a school, it is better to have none. Or perhaps the best solution is that of Hans Scharoun who has provided in the Geschwister-Schule of Lünen that the children shall themselves embellish the walls as they go along. The results are childlike and charming. Without any sentimentality about youth, it can be safely said that the work is at least as interesting as that of the adult professionals who have worked in other schools, and I happen to think considerably more meaningful. Some day, of course, the walls of Lünen will be filled up. But in the following summer a tactful covering over of the areas painted by those no longer there (though there are some sentimental risks for the alumni in this) could provide fresh

walls for new generations. It is a nice biological if antihistorical idea, which of course runs the risk of destroying an early work by some latter-day Dürer.

The adults' painting is more inept and inconsequential than downright bad. Most of the mosaics are weak and many are bad. There is a modest quality to the various anatomical panels which adorn the Apothecaries' Gardens in Hamburg, direct representations of that part of the human system for which a given group of plants is supposed to supply tonic or remedy. But Hans Leistikow's feeble glass mosaic frieze of figures from the Commedia dell' arte definitely mars the front of Gerhard Weber's National Theater in Mannheim, while a blank wall would have done more for the main stairwell of the Federal Ministry of the Interior in Bonn than Will Sohl's mediocre mosaic picture. Others are total disasters. There is, for instance, Erich Reuter's seven-story mosaic on the end of the City Saving Bank in Bonn, a combination of enormous triangles set apart by thin lines and filled in with highly colored pieces of natural stone and blue ceramics—a design which is loud and entirely incompatible with the architecture of the building itself, though no worse, I suppose, than most of the monumental documentary murals on the ends of buildings in Mexico City. A little better as a piece of design, though very overpowering in its room, is Bernd Krimmel's floor-to-floor mosaic for the foyer of the Federal Office for Statistics in Wiesbaden. The epitome of bad combinations is reached, however, in some of the exteriors of Rolf Gutbrod's Liederhalle in Stuttgart which is often so nice inside. Outside there is a wild array of ceramics and natural stones of many colors, many textures, and even many shapes and scales in what amounts to a shocking example of why building walls should not be too busy. The multiple forms of the Liederhalle offer enough problems without confounding them with this

83

81
Wolfsburg. Kulturzentrum.
Alvar Aalto

noisy and unpleasant overworking. We have seen a good deal of overworking of some of our own façades in the use of forms more appropriate to Venice or the seraglio but have escaped much flagrant mosaic application except in a few speculative housing developments. Let us hope that we can keep it so.

Indeed, by far the best mural I saw in Germany is an ensemble of enormous fossils taken from the great collection of Professor Haupt at Holzmaden, near Stuttgart, and mounted skillfully on the stair wall of the new and brilliant Parliament Building of Baden-Württemberg in Stuttgart. The great success of this piece of indigenous art and the equal success of Aalto's artful though art-less Kultur-zentrum at Wolfsburg makes one think again about the slogans of art in our time. Perhaps the artists and the architects really are incompatible today. Perhaps everybody should stop trying. But one thing is sure for both Germany and America, that it is better to have no art in architecture at all than bad art, weak art, meaningless art, irrelevant art. The question is whether the occasional rare successes excuse the myriad failures. I suppose in the end they do—but it would be nice if there were more successes.

Where the Heart Is

It is so obvious that it would be embarrassing to state it, were it not so often forgotten. Eliel Saarinen put it that a people gets the architecture it deserves. Ruskin argued that great architecture required at least a little extravagance, and that one would empty his purse only for things that he loved. The Temple of Ise would not be so meticulously rebuilt (foolishly, a businessman might say) periodically in the absence of some important Japanese conviction.

If this is so, it should not be expected that *all* the buildings of an age should be distinguished, even if some are. Nor should it be expected that the distinguished buildings of one country should necessarily be for the same purposes as those of another.

In a country as rich as the United States, it is, of course, likely that somewhere some client may be found to build a noble building for a purpose which moves him even though it does not move many of us. The isolated wonder like Tyrone Guthrie's theater in Minneapolis does not thereby become a mirror of the national purpose.

The same must be said for Gordon Bunshaft's beautiful Beinecke Rare Book Library at Yale. It must be an absolute delight for those bibliophiles who are enamored of the arts of the book, and it will distress the greater number of pedants who disdain every part of a book but its contents, or those who disdain collecting altogether, or the vastly larger number who are simply bewildered by or indifferent to the whole business. Thus its architecture is likely to be judged by its premises rather than by its magnificent achievement. It must be admitted it serves only a remote fragment of the national purpose but is not to be excommunicated on that ground.

Yet it may be easier for foreigners to detect the national purpose than it is for the nationals. They are less confused, perhaps, by contradictory knowledge. English critics have, for example, no difficulty in comprehending and castigating American architecture after very short and superficial exposures.

But even an American can notice things. One never forgets such a conversation as I had in a Pullman car perhaps fifteen years ago with the Republican chairman of the board of an important oil company who insisted that if Americans had wasted money on fountains as the Romans had, we would not now be in a position to rebuild the world. This was echoed five years ago by the almost contemptuous remark of a very self-assured Democratic foreign policy planner that it might be that Americans could not afford the extravagance of architecture in the next few years, there being so many other more important things to do, especially for one not very interested in the arts save as a tool of diplomatic conversation. These are, of course, threads from the same rug, a very old and not very handsome American rug.

And so it would not be hard to go on from this to try to decipher what kinds of architecture Americans might be willing to be extravagant about, were they willing to be extravagant about anything. (Now and again we are, of course, extravagant in architecture, but never without feeling embarrassed and apologetic.) I am not going to try to pursue this fairly obvious exercise which any American who keeps his eyes open can do for himself. This *is* a report on Germany. But it must be noted that the German trip did reemphasize for me the importance of a country having some architectural priorities, and the importance of having the right priorities.

This is not to say that all the German priorities are the right ones and all the American priorities wrong. But as we look at the German interests, I at least can feel regret that some of them are not better developed here.

On the whole I have no doubt that we build more interesting educational buildings at all levels, better hospitals, better airports, better libraries, better private houses. We have made many more interesting commercial buildings, and much larger ones, but the best German examples could be suggestive to us in their dignity, their modesty, and their relation to the other needs of the city. Art galleries are perhaps also a stand-off. The Germans have clearly done better than we in their group housing, their churches, their theaters, and other buildings for public recreation, and it is these types I will emphasize here.

There are isolated examples of excellent housing communities in our country, of course, going way back to Sunnyside, New York, and Radburn, New Jersey, and continuing through Chatham Village, Pennsylvania, and Baldwin Hills Village in California to Fresh Meadows, Long Island. The best of these so far have been of the low-rise English-village type, more consonant with our historic habits and tastes than the ultimately inevitable high-rise developments have seemed to be. It could be argued that if Continental Europeans have done better with such things than we, it is simply a consequence of urban history and time lag, and I hope this may be so. But the fact still is that we have few good high-rise developments and that most of our good ones, viewed in architectural terms, are to be found in privately or semiprivately financed projects, and all too often in high-rental units. On the other hand, most of our federally supported and supervised housing has been held to the grindstone of unimaginative, dreary, and overly institutionalized standards.

It does not take long to see that German rental housing, at almost every level save that of luxury, is not only more abundant but also more interesting and pleasant, whether the measure is that of comfortable interiors or simply how the units look on the cityscape.

The latter, of course, is not or should not be the dominant gauge for housing; but if it is left out, the housing and the city fall behind. There are naturally many dull housing arrangements in Germany, too; but they are not the norm, and as a lesson to us it is not important that individually better examples may be found in Scandinavia or occasionally in England.

There are no doubt reasons for this which go beyond architecture, but there is also a long-standing tradition. It stretches back at least to the ancient 82 Fuggerei in Augsburg which has happily been restored and which provides amiable if not spacious old people's housing almost in the middle of town. But there was also a great surge in the days of the Weimar Republic when excellent groups were put together, such as the Weissenhof Siedlung in Stuttgart and the Siedlungen Britz and Siemensstadt in Berlin, all engaging the attention of the very best German architects of their day.

Most of this pre-Hitlerian housing was of modest height, combining one- and two-story buildings with many of four and six, and never any towers. All of these were designed to supply verdure near the dwelling units and good climatic orientation. The great traditional quality has been preserved to a considerable extent in the postwar buildings and the new ingredient of high-rise has also entered into the brew, often brilliantly and seldom as tyrannically and coldly as the towers which stand, for example, in so many parts of the periphery of Paris or New York.

In most of the German buildings, the balcony plays a major role both in the life and in the appearance of the housing units. The inside rooms are pleasant but more compact than we would accept; and though the public lawns may be near and though there is much inclement weather, German tenants can be counted on to use the balconies intensively, to adorn them with appropriate furniture, sun shades, and umbrellas, and especially with geraniums and other vividly colored potted plants. Since the trees and public space are also well tended, the whole surrounding is infinitely more amiable than that to be found in most of our public housing (the Germans reserve asphalt pavements and meagre land maintenance for schools where we do somewhat better, at least in the suburbs).

Not all of the urban housing contains balconies, but those which do not have some other gesture

83 left

Mannheim. Apartment
house, Augusta-Anlage 17.
Emil Spickert, Horst Basel

84 right

Mannheim. Apartment
house, Gontardplatz.
Emil Spickert, Horst Basel

85
Berlin. Residential house,
Kottbusser Tor.
Wassili Luckhardt

86
Mannheim. Apartment
house, Zellstoff Waldhof.
Philipp Wolf

87
Essen. Apartment houses,
Goethestrasse.
Wilhelm Seidensticker

88
Berlin-Charlottenburg.
Apartment houses,
Goebelplatz.
Hans Scharoun

89
Berlin-Charlottenburg.
Unité d'habitation, "Typ
Berlin."
Le Corbusier

toward the outdoors and are likely to be individual, in-town buildings of greater luxury and expense such as the dwelling and business building built by Emil Spickert and Horst Basel on the Augusta Anlage in Mannheim. But even for the same purposes and given a little more room as they had on the Gontardplatz, the same architects began to lean toward balconies. Many German balconies are built into a structure, shielded by the walls and offering a flat though indented façade. A highly sophisticated but perhaps not very human version of this can be seen on Wassili Luckhardt's residential house at the Kottbusser Tor in Berlin. More typical, more useful, and I think more pleasant, is the apartment house by Philipp Wolf in Mannheim at Zellstoff Waldhof.

Still more typical and I think altogether the more ingratiating (as well as more traditional) are those which project firmly into the sun. Some of these are most cheerful and gay, such as the ones Wilhelm Seidensticker built on the Goethestrasse in Essen or the quite similar ones in the Calenberger Neustadt, Hanover. The ones in Molthanstrasse, Hanover, have the same idea, but the gaiety begins to be muted.

As the buildings of necessity go higher, the pleasant intimacy of the balconies seem to die away; they become more institutionalized, although, as some of the examples show, this is not inevitable. In many cases it is as though the form began to appeal to the architect more than the purpose. There is, for example, the kind of rigor to be found in Friedrick Blume's Golzheimer Terrace Houses in Düsseldorf. Although these balconies are too narrow, they are still quite good since they run across the whole flat. The balconies of Paul Schaeffer-Heyrothsberge have already become assertive in his apartment at Essen-Bredeney; while in Seidenstricker's higher Kaupenhöhe at Essen they hardly seem useful to the tenants what-

ever they may or may not do for the façade. The four-story housing for Siemens in Munich offers a reminder of what the balconies might have been, even when there is a great deal of concern for façade geometry. Scharoun, on the other hand, has shown that façaded balconies and gaiety are still possible in his combination of high- and low-rise apartments on the Goebelplatz in Charlottenburg Nord, Berlin.

Indeed, one of the sharpest tests of the designer of housing in Germany is how he manages the balcony problem. The average score is very high, and among the high scorers must be numbered Alvar Aalto in his two "Hochhauser," one in the Hansaviertel Berlin and the other at Neue Vahr, east of Bremen, to which I shall return.

A special case is that of Le Corbusier's dramatic and popular Unité d'Habitation near the Olympic Stadium in Berlin. Following the experience of Marseille and Nantes, Le Corbusier had well crystallized his thinking about this kind of enormous apartment involving 527 one-, two-, and three-room units. It was commissioned as part of the colossal effort at the Hansaviertel's International Exhibition of 1957, but it was much too large and much too spectacular to be put on a site with the other designs, so it was moved to a position of solitary eminence well outside Berlin, near to the Olympic Stadium and swimming pool. The German sponsors were skeptical that German tenants would accept duplexes or very low ceilings, but on these points Le Corbusier prevailed and was proved right. In a dispute with city authorities Le Corbusier lost the recreational and commercial floor at midheight he used at Marseille but retained the *pilotis*, his own sculpture, the incised statements, and especially the brilliant colors of the loges. It is an impressive building, and it is clear how a master can use small balconies well, almost like theater loges, while lesser men stick them on like the shells of a Spanish Baroque house in Salamanca. It is a pretty definite answer to the critics who have decried all the Unités on "human" functional grounds. These flats are small; the building is far from the center of urban life; it is some distance from all the usual minor amusements and even serious shopping; indeed, its only nearby asset is the great outdoor Olympic pool which in the Berlin climate is usable only a few months each year. The Hansaviertel, on the other hand, is convenient to everything and many of its buildings, too, are pleasant. But of all the housing in Berlin, I am told, the Unité has the longest waiting list except for Aalto's building in the Hansaviertel; and this is not a matter of the rental cost.

One more and quite different example of unusual housing is the apartment cluster Romeo und Julia by Hans Scharoun in Zuffenhausen on the northern outskirts of Stuttgart. Here the master is at his capricious best, providing a lively and sharply differentiated environment.

Our architects and public administrators could learn a great deal about the design of community housing from a trip through Germany. But buildings alone do not constitute housing. Grouping is equally important, and here too the German performance has been generally good, if not often reaching the brilliant combination Mies van der Rohe effected long ago at Weissenhof in Stuttgart.

The old dignified arrangements of Siemensstadt and Britz seem to be more "human" in scale and arrangement than some of the new projects, just as Welwyn and Letchworth seem more livable than Britain's new New Towns. This may be the effect of time which, given a hand, produces grass and trees. One is a little uneasy about so simple an answer, though. Why, for example, are Gropius' contributions to Siemensstadt in 1929 clearly superior to TAC's at Hansaviertel in 1957? Was the problem simpler then, if only in terms of numbers? Is there something about our life that caused the architects to create an arrangement in 1957 that lacked the sense of stability and repose apparent in the solution in 1929? Yet there are examples of new work adjoining old that do not lead to such a conclusion.

New arrangements such as Scharoun's additions to Bartning's work in Siemensstadt are in sympathy with the old; even Norman Braun's mottled buildings on the Otto-Suhr Allee seem to have the right quality.

The problem of combining high-rise with ground-hugging buildings has never been easy to solve gracefully. It may yet prove to be a bad theory. But about as bad an example as you are likely to find in Germany is the towers in the Siemens group in Munich, which as a city has had few entrancing encounters with contemporary architecture; by our measure this also is quite good.

We have nothing as amusing as Hansaviertel, almost in the center of Berlin. On an absolute scale there is much to criticize in Hansaviertel. It has a thoughtless street pattern and badly needed the kind of over-all control Mies provided at Weissenhof. Not all the buildings are good buildings. In many senses it was an exotic venture. On a piece of prime land in the central city, just around the corner from the Tiergarten, the Germans went all out to make a display. They invited the best-known architects from many parts of the world. They invited more than one American, but all the Americans except Gropius professed to be too busy; and this may have been just as well since so few of our best serious men, other than Neutra, Sert, Stubbins, and Pei, have paid much effective attention to housing. So in a sense the Hansaviertel was a fair and a competition; and one can be led to thinking of the buildings as trying to out-

91
Berlin-Charlottenburg.
Grosssiedlung Siemensstadt,
Bartning-Anban apartments.
Hans Scharoun

90
Stuttgart. Apartment
cluster, Romeo und Julia.
Two views.
Hans Scharoun

shout one another. But this is not, I think, in the end a just impression. Many of the buildings are genuinely distinguished; and somehow there is a reasonable cohesion between the rigid geometry of Schneider-Esleben and Hubert Hoffmann in Objekts 9 and 10, the planned chaos of Pierre Vago's balconies, the color if not the shape of TAC's Objekt 7, the coldness of Egon Eiermann's Objekt 13, the domestic dignity of Kay Fisker's low buildings, and Aalto's popular Objekt 16 which has intimations of his later tower at Bremen. The churches fit in well, though individually ugly, as do Zinsser's subway station, restaurant, and cinema, Paul Baumgarten's neat library, and Werner Düttmann's excellent Academy of Art. From the top of the highest house by Müller-Rehm to the lowest one, the atrium houses of Arne Jacobsen, I found it pleasant to be in the Hansaviertel and went back more than once though it is obviously a *tour de force*. I felt this even of the buildings I did not like very much, such as the mottled one by Eugène Beaudouin and Raymond Lopez, the honeycomb of van den Broek and Bakema, Sergius Ruegenberg's eccentric house, or Niemeyer's uncharacteristic and not very stylish or sensible unit.

Hansaviertel is almost certain to be disapproved of by orderly minds, whether they are housers or designers. But the test is whether it would be more pleasant to live in one of the wild buildings of the Hansa quarter, a building quite unlike that of your neighbor, or in one of the usual neat, orderly projects. In the end one has to vote for Hansa although one may wonder how many Hansas a single city could manage to provide before they had lost their exciting quality. Probably only one, and the lesson of Hansa must be the same as that Alvar Aalto used to impress on students—at least you should keep trying to "let the bear get in the window," to search for variety without caprice.

But you will have to settle, no doubt, for less caprice than the Hansaviertel.

On the whole a good example of what may be possible is the enormous and generally excellent Neue Vahr on the eastern outskirts of Bremen, a very large combination of two-story and four-story buildings with others of eight and fourteen, and dominated by the twenty-two-story Hochhaus of Alvar Aalto. Not all the architecture is distinguished, but little of it is bad. There is a great play of color, and different quarters are easily found and identified. The most distinguished building is clearly Aalto's though it may by its refinement overshadow the others too much. Also, it is nearest the community center and the delightful artificial pond, so things may be more pleasant there than they are on the periphery. But it is hard to find fault with Neue Vahr save in one respect, the respect in which the others fail, too. This is that these complexes, though they do have schools and churches and shopping centers, seem to be deficient in the total opportunity to do community things such as one finds offered in Scandinavia or at Roehampton, England, and even, though in a duller way, in Harlow and Stevenage. Perhaps this will come later; perhaps it is deliberately omitted to bring people willy-nilly back to the center city even for things the village could provide. Perhaps it is not the German way of life. But I felt it to be the principal, perhaps the only, defect in the enormous physical achievement of the German rebuilders.

It has been enormous. So far the following units have been built in Berlin alone (I speak only of the big estates): Charlottenburg, 3,700; Britz South, 3,284; Schillerhöhe in Wedding, 2,078; George Ramin, 1,321; Tegel, 1,192; Mariendorf, 761—a total of 12,336. To come soon are Britz-Buckow-Rudow, 15,500, and Spandau, 6,000, a grand total of 33,000-odd units in the big congeries

92
Berlin-Tiergarten.
Hansaviertel.
Paul Schneider-Esleben

93
Berlin-Tiergarten.
Hansaviertel.
Pierre Vago

94
Berlin-Tiergarten.
Hansviertel.
The Architects Collaborative

95
Berlin-Tiergarten.
Hansviertel.
Egon Eiermann

96
Berlin-Tiergarten.
Hansaviertel.
Kay Fisker

97
Berlin-Tiergarten.
Hansaviertel.
Alvar Aalto

98 far left

Berlin-Tiergarten.
Hansviertel.

Eugène Beaudouin,
Raymond Lopez

99 left

Berlin-Tiergarten.
Hansaviertel.

J. H. van den Broek,
J. B. Bakema

100

Berlin-Tiergarten.
Hansaviertel.

Oscar Niemeyer

101b
Neue Vahr skyscraper.

101
Bremen. Neue Vahr.
Alvar Aalto

101a
Neue Vahr apartment
buildings.

alone. Faced with numbers like this, the Mexicans have built grim prison cities like the new one at Nonoalco, the French have spattered the periphery of Paris with anonymous high buildings rising from the mud, and the Americans have simply continued to flow out and over the truck gardens of the East and the walnut and artichoke plantations of the West.

Others might depart from a German visit with less enthusiasm than I about site planning in the housing, but I doubt that anyone would question the quality of the architectural performance.

Naturally, one wonders why their achievement in group housing has been so strong. It is true that the bureaucracies are less timid. Yet much of their housing has been achieved through the use of private capital under an ingenious limited-dividend-cum-tax-alleviation system; thus the variety in the housing there is a consequence of private initiative as well as the good taste of the bureaucracies. It is true that the Germans are used to more compact living: Most would not prefer a ranchhouse in the latest desolate development in Marin County or on Long Island to an orderly row house in Hansaviertel or Neue Vahr. It is true that they are not so suspicious of the "public domain" and that their land controls are more effective and less debated. As the upshot of all these forces, and as a result too of their habits of mind, housing has engaged the attention of all the leading German architects as it has not engaged the attention of many of ours, who find greater profits and more acclaim in other design activities. It seems to me a cause for embarrassment that our great architectural task forces could muster but one contributor to the Hansaviertel.

But in this as in other things architectural, the straw reveals the wind. If we Americans do not demand much pleasant public housing, we can hardly blame architects for not spending their best efforts on it.

One turns to the same explanation for the obvious fact that German theaters and churches are also much better than ours.

If the architects are the great leaders we presuppose them to be, or at least that they claim to be, one might wonder why the Clarence Steins and the Henry Churchills and the Percival Goodmans and more recently the Ieoh Ming Peis have, for all their dedication, affected us so little. It is not even a puzzlement, as the King of Siam used to worry.

Except for Harry Weese's Arena Stage in Washington, Ralph Rapson's theater for Tyrone Guthrie in Minneapolis, perhaps Philip Johnson's controversial Ballet Theater in New York, and Clowes Memorial Hall at Butler University, Indianapolis, by John Mac Johansen, there are no American examples that are comparable to the theaters of Mannheim, Münster, and Gelsenkirchen, the opera house at Cologne or even the more conventional one in Berlin, to say nothing of Scharoun's new Concert Hall of the Berlin Philharmonic, the Liederhalle in Stuttgart, even the relatively dull Beethovenhalle in Bonn. As places of general assembly one can think of the Congress Hall in Berlin (by the American architect Stubbins), the Gürzenich in Cologne, the special sports hall Gruga in Essen, and the market and exhibition halls everywhere, but perhaps most noteworthy the Rhein-Main-Halle in Wiesbaden.

Certainly we do not compare favorably with the German achievement if we must cite Frank Lloyd Wright's disasters in Dallas and Phoenix; the clumsy, if functional, campus theaters of Harrison and Abramowitz; the inflexible auditorium at M.I.T.; the vulgar contemporary version of the Diamond Horseshoe conceived in other terms that is emerging at Lincoln Center in New York; or the vulgar "Pavilion" in the new Los Angeles Music Center, at whose opening, a performance of Resphighi's "Roman Festivals" seemed entirely appropriate to the architecture. The fact is that any American architect has to deal with an attitude toward opera which is essentially one of fancy dress. The ushers at Los Angeles wear Nehru coats and hats, and the coats are "orchid-raspberry" and orange-red—what fun! As long as American opera houses have to be endowed with private Founders Rooms, as long as reporters are more interested in who came to the opera and what they wore than what was sung and how, we cannot expect that our opera houses and theaters will match those of Germany any more than what is done inside them matches the German accomplishment.

The greatest disasters are not always evident architecturally. The Metropolitan Opera Company, for example, cannot afford to bring its expensive productions to Boston except in a big hall; and the available big hall, seating 6,000, is in a convention barn in the new Prudential Center. Thus it might even be an artistic gain for Boston if the Metropolitan Opera were to stay at home and that city had more support to give to its own modest but serious opera company. That, it must be said, would be the German solution.

We must not forget that each of the good American examples cited performs an exotic function while the great German theaters and opera houses serve an almost routine one, the daily taken-for-granted offering over many months of a rich repertoire of operatic or theatrical performances based chiefly on resident directors, producers, and companies.

In some cities, it may be the theater which is more successful and better known outside the city limits; in others, the opera. Some, like Hamburg, are distinguished for both. But this is not the point. Either or both, the people of most German cities are supporting six or eight performances of theater or opera a week over a season of nine or more months. Because of the rivalries between cities, most of the support is local and this means it is possible for a German city of half a million to keep something going that is achieved here only in a few cities which enjoy the dubious benefit of a season of New York tryouts followed later by second-line casts in the successful plays, and a short conventional visit by the Metropolitan Opera Company.

The repertory of opera in any of these cities is

wider and more interesting than that available in New York; and the theatrical repertory includes a far larger number of classics and fewer one-night flops.

The word support needs elaboration. It means on the one hand that enough local people will buy tickets day by day at moderate prices to come near to filling a hall that seats some 1,200 to 1,800, the usual German size (Berlin's is 1,900), and a good size aesthetically. The ticket sales do not meet the cost of production, to be sure, and behind the success there is invariably a subsidy, mainly provided by the city. Americans tend to dismiss the German success with a sneer at the subsidy as though anything which is free is bound to look successful if only the attendant crowds are measured. This is, of course, fallacious: A crowd coming only because it has nothing else to do and because the event is free could not display the interest and sophistication that the German theater and opera audiences do. Moreover, the subsidy comes from taxes which Germans happily pay because they want theater and opera.

In *Die Welt,* Hamburg, for Saturday, September 21, 1963, houses in 36 different German cities and towns as large as Berlin, Cologne, and Munich and as small as Hildesheim or Oldenburg listed about 200 different performances for the next week. Of these, 124 were of opera or ballet. They included 65 different pieces by 34 different composers. No opera was listed more than four times (4 each of *Fidelio, Magic Flute, Cosi Fan Tutte, Don Giovanni, Traviata, Rigoletto,* and *The Flying Dutchman*). The most frequent composers were Verdi (21 performances of 10 different operas); Mozart (14 performances of 5 different operas); Wagner (11 performances of 5 different operas); and Puccini (7 performances of 5 different operas); but there was a wide range of less familiar operas from Gluck to Berg, and fairly frequent representations of Rossini, Strauss, Mussorgsky, Smetana, and so on. The "big" Wagner operas such as *Parsifal* and *The Ring* were not included and *Tristan* only once. This amazing offering will normally continue everywhere through about a thirty-week season, over and above the special festivals such as Bayreuth's. The subsidies are substantial, amounting sometimes to as much as 23 marks a seat per performance which might add up to one and a half million dollars a year from the public purse in a city like West Berlin, reaching toward the financial inducements some American cities seem to have offered the owners of professional baseball clubs.

I do not know whether Americans want theater and opera (or flower boxes and balconies, or fountains, or handsome benches, or any of the many other amenities of civilization they do not have), but I do know that too little effort is being made to find out. It is perfectly evident that the febrile, speculative, commercial, vulgar approach of Broadway and the overly costly productions of the Metropolitan Opera do not give the American people much chance to find out, and they never will find out until each city learns to pay only a modest obeisance to New York. The San Francisco Opera has a more interesting repertoire and offers on the whole a more European experience but is essentially in the same line of *chichi* patronage as New York on a quieter scale. Yet San Francisco repeated in more cities would do more for America than touring companies of the Metropolitan. Of course, other countries have the same problem. To paraphrase Villon, "Il n'y a bon théâtre qu'a de Paris." But Germany shows a different way.

It must be the German desire for good theater and opera and the German willingness to make it generally available through urban subvention that has resulted in the good theaters and opera houses

102
Gelsenkirchen. State Theater.
Werner Ruhnau

103
Mannheim. National Theater.
Gerhard Weber

104
Münster. State Theater.
Harald Deilmann

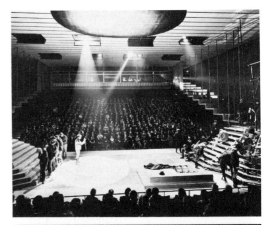

to be found everywhere in the Federal Republic.

A national mood cannot be invented or even awakened by all the largess of The Ford Foundation if the latent hope is not genuine and widespread. If it does some day manifest itself in more theaters and opera houses in our country, they probably should be contemporary in design but not because this in itself guarantees a finer experience. As I said earlier, there is no more attractive place to go to opera than in the little baroque Theater of the Residence in Munich (created by François Cuvilliés le Vieux, 1751–1753). The experience is excellent in Düsseldorf, or Hanover, or Hamburg, each of which has either an old theater building or a modern one which is in no way spectacular. It may be a little disconcerting or even offensive to contemporary doctrinaires to be told that this is so. But it is.

Apart from the performance, there are certain pleasures and conveniences associated with the theater—entering it, leaving one's coat, finding one's seat, hearing and seeing, enjoying a comfortable and pleasing foyer, bar, or restaurant between acts— which have been well provided in Germany for a long time. The contemporary theaters may do these as well as the old; their contemporaneity is no guarantee that they will do them better.

All German theaters take good care of your arrival. You proceed at once to a designated checkroom related to your seat number and check quickly without waiting in line. You proceed with equal ease to your seat. Most likely you will be in a loge or box and will be one of only eight people who will use a door to that particular area. If you are sitting on the main floor, it will be in a wide row extending from side aisle to side aisle, but again only a few rows will be served by one entrance. The absence of a central aisle would doubtless not be permitted here by some fire laws, would compound the nuisance of our late arrivals, and is

already objected to at Lincoln Center. In Germany the people care enough for the theater to get there on time; to enjoy it they do not have to have three cocktails first; and if they are going to eat a large meal, they do it after the performance is over. All this the architect can count on—and his problem here is to provide smooth and quick circulation at all points, plus, of course, reasonable sight and sound lines within.

The new German houses abound in foyers and visible stairs and encourage movement up and down—they have not yet come to escalators, let alone elevators. An immediately noticeable difference between the old and new theaters is that the new do not close the spectacle in; rather they encourage its display to those who are not in the theater but in the street. Theatergoers are exposed to the public at Münster, although this is not the main element of the design, which is the curved enclosure of auditorium and stage. It is an important element of Bornemann's design for the Berlin Opera House, and it is the transcendent element of Ruhnau's theater at Gelsenkirchen. (It has been largely missed so far at Lincoln Center, but not completely.) Perhaps this is more appropriate to modern ways and dress. Yet it is not majestically different from, for example, the Grand Escalier in the Opera House in Paris, save that the display is no longer private. In some designs the balconies are a dominant part of the composition of the auditorium. At Hanover the seats are provided in conventional rings. The seating is not an important part of the impression at Mannheim though the open stairs at the sides of the little theater are spectacular. There are many and prominent balconies at Münster, but they are not very obtrusive partly because of the shape of the hall and partly because of the strange and restless ceiling. The balconies have become quite dramatic at Hamburg, and the boxes in Berlin as well. In

106
Berlin-Charlottenburg.
Apartment houses,
Otto-Suhr-Allee.
Norman Braun

107
Cologne. Opera House.
Wilhelm Riphahn

105
Berlin. Opera House.
*Rebuilt according to design
by Fritz Bornemann*

Berlin it is hard to avoid comparing the boxes with the balconies to be found, for example, on Norman Braun's housing on the Otto-Suhr-Allee in Charlottenburg. Boxes in the Cologne Opera House are most insistent, as they protrude in the staggered tobogganlike tiers. The treatment of these seating arrangements is still in development, and it is hard to say whether it will move away from the extremes of Cologne. I expect it will if only because there are other designers than Ruhnau who are thinking more in theatrical terms than in those that concern the comfort of the audience in intermission.

The National Theater in Mannheim, for example, impressed me as an actors' and producers' theater; the two stages work easily with one another with some inconvenience to the spectator when entering or during intermission. Once in the auditorium, the main experience should be sharply focused on stage, and I suppose ideally in the view of its designer, Gerhard Weber, the illusion would not be shattered at intermission. When the auditorium is darkened and the stage is at work, the novel techniques offer an ease of concentration, but this involvement turns into a fairly depressing social experience when the house lights are up.

The small house at Gelsenkirchen shows this in the extreme. The balcony hangs free in space. The side walls are used for lights or actions, not for audience. The floor may hold audience or actors or both. A small orchestra ditch can be shut and a proscenium erected, providing what Ruhnau calls a "peephole" theater. If the proscenium is removed, a full room platform theater results, the stage served from above and the sides. The foyer window is curtained to create a sense of total enclosure. The stage can also be put in the middle of the floor to create an arena theater. Actors then enter from folding walls on the side which also emits the light. A light bridge is dropped above the

platform, and the technical needs of the stage are managed from above. The foyer curtains are opened. Or the theater may be mobile with several platforms, achieving "an optimal integration" of actors and spectators. Gelsenkirchen is the best realized step to the totally mobile theater of which Ruhnau dreams.

Stagecraft does change as well as producers' views as to the relation between audience and stage, so the greatest differences between the old theater, for example, and the new rests here. But it may be a mistake to believe that the new experimental theaters can do everything better than the traditional theater. The truth probably is that they do some things better and some things less well. There is no such thing as absolute flexibility. When you tear down the proscenium you have gained some liberties, but you cannot get the proscenium back with a wave of the hand—even if there, visually it may not feel solid as a good old-fashioned fourth wall or picture frame should.

Given such a degree of interest and experiment in the theater resting on a long tradition of the same, it is not surprising that German theaters and opera houses offer important elements of the cityscape as they seldom do here. This is evident at Mannheim, at Cologne, at Münster, and, of course, at Gelsenkirchen.

Ernst May called the new Münster theater, inaugurated in February 1956, an emancipating clap of thunder; Wallace Harrison is supposed to have said in substance that he had seen theaters all over the world from Moscow to Rio de Janeiro but he had never seen a more beautiful theater than that of Münster. The experience did not seem to affect the designers of Lincoln Center.

If we do not get as good theaters as the Germans, it may largely be because we do not want them so much rather than because our architects cannot design well enough. The method of selecting the

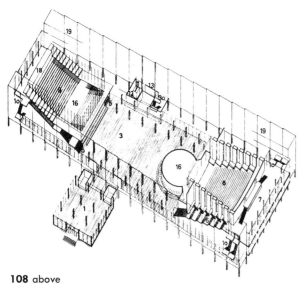

108 above

Mannheim. National
Theater. Isometric view.

1 Box office
3 Lobby
5 Stairways to the
  auditorium
6 Stairways to the
  balconies
7 Foyer, large theater
8 Auditorium, large
  theater
9 Auditorium, small
  theater
10 Emergency exits
11 Utility room
12 Passenger elevator
13 Freight elevator
16 Main stage
18 Foyer, small theater
30 Stairways

Gerhard Weber

109 below and opposite

Gelsenkirchen. State
Theater. The Little Theater.
Pictorial, graphic views of
mobile stage.

Walter Ruhnau

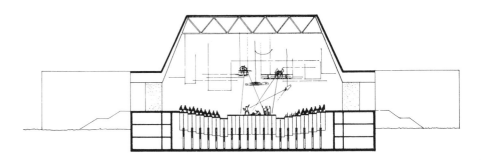

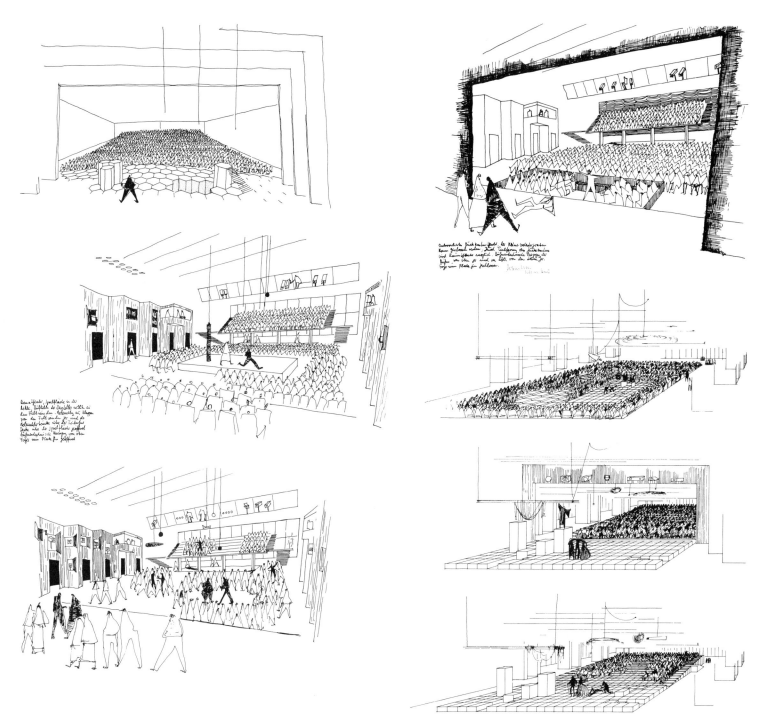

110
Mannheim. National
Theater.
Gerhard Weber

111
Cologne. Opera House.
Wilhelm Riphahn

Münster. State Theater.
Harald Deilmann

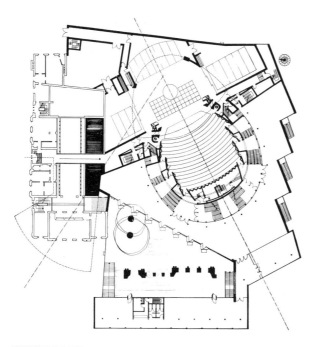

113
Bonn. Beethoven Hall.

114
Stuttgart. Concert Hall.
Floor plan.
Rolf Gutbrod

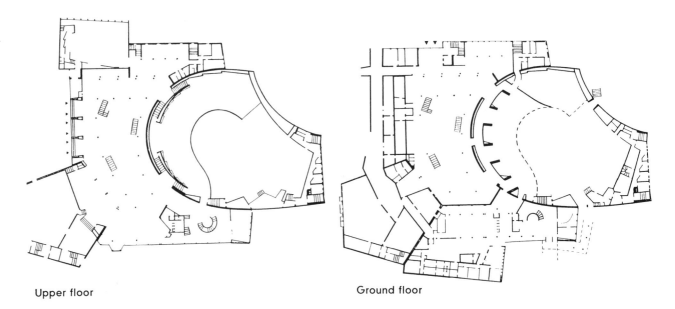

Upper floor   Ground floor

designer may play a role. Competitions are not suitable for every American building project. But they would be eminently suitable for important theaters and concert halls.

Surely a competition could not have been less productive for Lincoln Center than the arrangement finally made. Have we not by now seen enough failures in the effort to "coordinate" a group of talented individuals, from United Nations to Lincoln Center, to be unwilling to trust this way any longer? A group of buildings such as those at Lincoln Center would have been better at the hand of Saarinen, Bunshaft, or Johnson, anyone of whom was capable of making a masterwork there, than as a consequence of the troika rig uneasily held together by a coordinator.

It is probable that we do at least as well at concertgoing as the Germans, and certainly we have more first-rate orchestras. There is, however, a somewhat different attitude in Germany. A concert may be regarded as a little more fun there. You can eat and drink well in most of the German concert halls. The Beethovenhalle at Bonn is reminiscent in principle but not detail of the Royal Festival Hall in London. We have no match for either in pleasure—least of all in the pseudosophisticated, snobbish, new Philharmonic in New York—but not in Boston's ritualistic and soporific Symphony Hall, either. The Beethovenhalle is not a very distinguished architectural monument, but it sits in a pleasant park and its terraces look out over the ever interesting Rhine. Within there are the usual generous foyers and two halls, large and small, each with a good deal of flexibility in seating, influenced somewhat perhaps by broadcasting-studio technique. Chairs are comfortable, aisles generous, acoustics live, so it is fun to go to a concert there, resembling neither an occasion on which your attendance is supposed to be noted as a matter of social distinction nor a sort of reverential approach to music and musicians.

The much publicized Liederhalle in Stuttgart is even more interesting. If the exterior is bizarre and confusing, the inside though strange is more convincing from the characteristically gay and expansive foyers to the kidney-shaped asymmetrical auditorium in which the curves of room and balcony play contrapuntally and in which it is possible to modify seating as wished. The smaller concert hall is more stark but at least as interesting. Both work well musically.

Scharoun's Philharmonic Hall in Berlin, dedicated in September 1963, carries the Stuttgart idea still further. The foyers are full of changes of pace as stairs and platforms and walls cooperate to give always new visual sensations as one walks through. This is a fitting preparation for the fantastic asymmetrical hall in which about a third of the audience sits behind the orchestra so that a symphony hall has become in some senses a concert hall in the round. This would seem to offer some technical difficulties. For example, it would seem impossible to position the various choirs of the orchestra so that they could present roughly the same experience to all parts of the hall. Perhaps the leader finds what he likes and then sticks to it; but guest conductors have different views and Karajan, who approved the design, will not conduct forever. On the funny side, but not to be dismissed as totally irrelevant, is the fact that about one third of the audience can now see the facial expressions of the conductor, an unhappy invitation to distracting showmanship. It happens now that a New York reviewer, not liking Bernstein's reading of a score, may remark that his footwork was nonetheless impeccable. What further openings this arrangement offers to the Berlin musicians and their reviewers who may not have seen a symphony on television!

115
Berlin-Tiergarten. Concert
Hall of the Berlin
Philharmonic.
Hans Scharoun

The acclaim for the musical conditions at the opening seems to have been as hearty as the complaints were about new orchestral ambiance in Lincoln Center. The exterior of the Philharmonic, as is typical of all of Scharoun's buildings, follows the interior without compromise and is jerky, lacking much charm. But as the librarian is supposed to have offered as an inscription for Yale's Stirling Library, what matters is inside!

There are other interesting halls in Germany. The Rhein-Main-Halle in Wiesbaden, very large, very comfortable, very efficient, has considerable dignity. But though it looks large and is certainly more elegant than our sports arenas, it is in fact much smaller, seating only 4,200 at boxing, for example, as compared with 13,000 and more in our halls. The Grugahalle in Essen offers special and interesting facilities for sports or even religious congregations and is more attractive than our present installations in the Gardens of Boston and Madison Square.

Its alar shape, dictated largely by the structure of the stands (and similar to the new hall at Bremen), is dramatic if not beautiful. The well-known Congress Hall in Berlin, by Hugh Stubbins, serves its purposes far better and far more pleasantly than anyone will dream who has not seen it. The foyers and rooms of the Gürzenich in Cologne are plush and gay. So the accomplishment in this area is high, too, if perhaps not unique.

Occasionally this is true also of the great trade exhibition establishments. The one in Düsseldorf is certainly cheerful and of some architectural quality. On the other hand, the equally famous grouping at Dortmund is positively grimy, while the large area at Hanover is spotted with unfortunate installations. In the end, the cultural halls in Germany, and probably the sports halls as well, can offer us something to think about while the commercial halls, more important to their life

than to ours, are with the possible exception of Rhein-Main in Wiesbaden, not worth an architectural visit. It is also noticeable and perhaps surprising that a country whose people are such competent engineers offers so few flights of engineering fancy. There are few, perhaps there are no building engineering achievements in Germany which attain the power and beauty of Nervi's or for that matter of Nowicki's stock pavilion, Eero Saarinen's TWA, his Yale Hockey Rink, or Dulles International Airport; of course, Buckminster Fuller is unique. Our building engineering is more interesting than what is in evidence in Germany today. But still Essen and Bremen and Wiesbaden have the pleasant new public spaces denied to many American cities in the midst of their affluent and destructive redevelopment.

The situation is even clearer in other sorts of municipal recreational buildings. They are better designed, more amusing, less institutional, and better kept. The swimming baths are extraordinary almost everywhere. They are almost always a combination of park, restaurants, glass to let in lots of sun, several pools for people of different ages and talents and for groups such as families and for individuals. Otto Fischer's at Frankfurt/M. Höchst has typically gay decor and a vibrant "Schmuckhof." The Tullabad at Karlsruhe has the usual and decorative array of diving boards which have always interested architects. Berlin has many pleasant pools and especially good ones at Reinickendorf and Wilmersdorf. There is an impressive one not far from the Cathedral in Cologne. The concrete and glass structure of Frankfurt's Central Indoor Swimming Pool is strong, clear, and comfortable. The Fössebad complex outside Hanover involves public indoor and outdoor baths, schools of various levels, playing fields, a church, and a Freizeitheim all quite near the Leine. Everyone will find his own favorite,

116
Essen. Gruga Hall.
Exterior by day,
surrounded by litter; and
by night, surrounded by
cars.
E. F. Brickmann,
G. Lichtenhahn

117
Bremen. Kulturzentrum.

118
Berlin. Congress Hall.
Hugh Stubbins

119
Cologne. Gürzenich.
Foyer.
Rudolf Schwarz, Karl Band

121
Essen. Neu Hauptbad.
P. F. Schneider

122
Hanover-Linden.
Freizeitheim.

121 but the three combined pools in the new Hauptbad at Essen seemed to me the most charming. We know how to make such things, I am sure, but for all our affluence we do not often achieve them; and it is not often that our municipal establishments remain clean, cheerful, and inviting, or appealing to citizens of many economic and social classes.

I must pass quickly over the fine array of hostels, youth centers, leisure centers, housing for single persons. The emphasis is always that leisure can be combined with nature, with health, with athletics, and with learning. It is not beneath the dignity or the budget of so distinguished an architect as Harald Deilmann to design a modest youth center in Münster. Erich Morgenroth did not hesitate to work on the simple youth hostel at the Pastoratsberg in Essen, a sensitive dormitory and recreation center that cannot be explained and must be seen. Werner Düttmann did the youth center at Berlin Zehlendorf. Hanover's first 122 Freizeitheim is an example of the more elegant arrangements. It is a sober Miesian shell containing libraries, shops, game rooms, and places to dance for many ages, laid out with efficiency, skill, beauty, and boldly combining the practical with the caprice of sculpture; it was designed by the municipal architectural office. Alvar Aalto's 81 analogous Kulturzentrum at Wolfsburg is more "swish" and here or there has delightfully characteristic Aalto touches and a fine library, but I am not sure it is really any better. A great deal of German social architecture is very well conceived, to the point where comparisons are embarrassing for us.

There is one other area in which comparisons are equally embarrassing. The German churches excel ours by a long stretch. There have, of course, been some pleasant and reverent churches built in our country in the same time. There were the early West-Coast churches of Belluschi; Wurster's excellent synagogue in Dallas; the collaborations of the Saarinens, father and son, in Minneapolis and in Columbus, Indiana; Eero Saarinen's Kresge Chapel at M.I.T. in Cambridge, and his last church, the well-tuned North Christian Church in Columbus, Indiana; and on the strong side, Breuer's Abbey Chapel at Collegeville, Minnesota. And there have been a number of near misses like the three chapels at Brandeis by Abramowitz; but for the most part, our churches have not come off well when they have departed from established conventions, and we have, on the one hand, too many weary A-frames and, on the other hand, too many demonstrations by the architect that he was about to prove that he knew how to be different. Frank Lloyd Wright was guilty of this in his late churches and synagogues; so was Louis Kahn when he built a kind of Egyptian tomb complex for the Unitarians in Rochester, New York; this was the fault of Anshen and Allen when they cast up a modern precast version of camp-meeting tents for the Methodists at Stockton, California; or Victor Lundy in his striving and bizarre First Unitarian Congregational Church at Hartford, Connecticut; or Curtis and Davis when they conceived the ostentatious St. Frances Cabrini in New Orleans. Naturally, some equally egregious, perhaps even more egregious, examples can be found in Germany; and one does have first to dispose of the vexing question whether what looks unfortunate in one's own situation might look more exciting somewhere else. I think this is not so and that the situation is indeed clear that there are only a handful of American churches which have the strength and restraint of fifty or more German churches built in the last seventeen years—and many more if one were to include the fine edifices of Otto Bartning and Dominikus Böhm of the pre-Hitlerian early thirties. The facts seem incontrovertible. A plausible explanation, or group of explanations, is elusive.

Many of the buildings were the outcome of competitions but not enough to prove much. It is a little too easy to say that there just happened to be a small cadre of talented architects in Germany in this moment who devoted their talents to church building. This is partially true. Of the forty churches which seem to me on reflection to be most worth remembering, almost a half are by Schwarz, the Böhms, Bartning, and Oesterlen, in that order. But there remain the twenty-one other churches by no fewer than seventeen different architects.

One looks for a common approach to the problem of designing a church such as was evident in Romanesque times but finds none unless it be broadly philosophical. There is no common approach to the plan, although the largest number are probably one-aisled rectangles with a flat wall at the end, or two flat walls to form a triangular apse or the conventional semicircular apse. But there are many other effective shapes, octagons, hexagons, pentagons, squares, circles (happily, no symbolic fish shapes and very few cruciform). There are rectangular plans with side aisles. Occasionally there are transepts. The Rochus-kirche in Düsseldorf by Schneider-Esleben has three hemicircular lobes. There are cruciform plans with three apses. St. Michael's in Frankfurt, by Rudolf Schwarz, is an oval with two oval chapels springing from near the altar. Allerheiligen by Alois Giefer and Hermann Mäckler, also in Frankfurt, is parabolic with rectangular wings

123

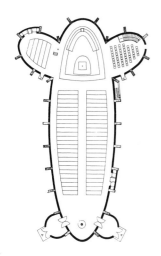

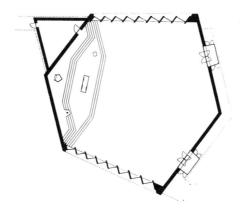

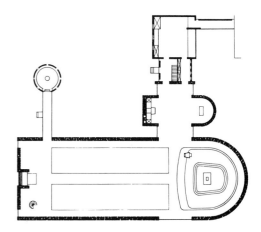

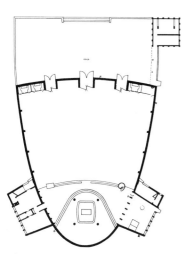

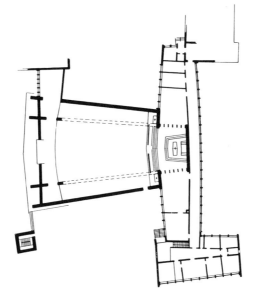

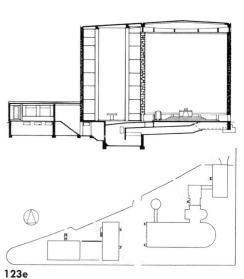

123a
Frankfurt. St. Michael's.
Rudolf Schwarz

123b
Frankfurt.
Allerheiligenkirche.
*Alois Giefer,
Hermann Mäckler*

123c
Unterrath. Evangelical
Church.
*Helmut Hentrich,
Hubert Petschnigg*

123d
Würzburg. St. Alfons'.
Hans Schädel

123e
Frankfurt. St. Wendel's.
Johannes Krahn

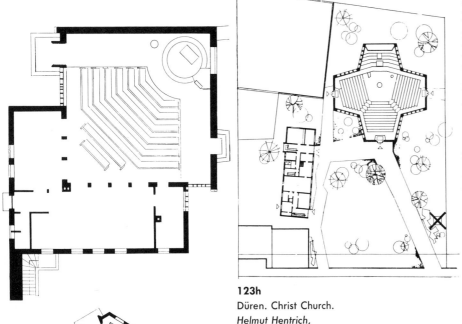

123h
Düren. Christ Church.
*Helmut Hentrich,
Hans Heuser*

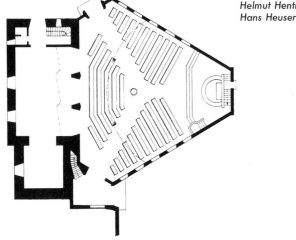

123f
Manching. Evangelical
Church.
Olaf Gulbrannsson

123g
Schwebheim. Evangelical
Church.
Olaf Gulbrannsson

near the altar. Helmut Hentrich and Hubert Petschnigg's Evangelischekirche at Unterrath is an irregular hexagon; and the Christuskirche at Düren by Hentrich and Heuser is a Greek cross with arms whose sides diverge from outside to inside. There are at least half a dozen more eccentric and freer forms, such as Schädel used at St. Alfons', Würzburg.

Furthermore, there are no fundamental agreements within the basic plan. The altar may be in an apse, against a solid wall, against a transparent wall, standing on axis or eccentrically, standing free like an arena stage at the focus of a curve, and, rarely, in the exact center of everything. There is no conventional position for choir or organ or pulpit; there may or may not be balconies.

Most of the churches give a high and light impression but some, like Baumgarten's Kirche am Lietzensee, Wilhelm Hesse and Leonhard Schulze's Lukaskirche in Cologne-Flittard, Oesterlen's Martinskirche in Hanover, or Bartning's Luther-Notkirche in Cologne-Mülheim, are relatively low; and others, like Schilling's St. Alban's on the Stadtgarten at Cologne or Striffler's Evangelische Trinitätiskirche at Mannheim are quite dark, at least on first entrance.

Nor is there any penchant for a particular material. Bricks, wood, metal, glass, concrete, glass-concrete, all the usual churchly materials except stone are used. The materials are exactly the ones architects are using here except for local differences in brick and the mason's craft, and except for the occasional sentimental reuse of the rubble of a destroyed building as when Schilling employed the bricks from the old Cologne opera house in the new St. Alban's or the Böhms poured the concrete side walls of St. Anna's in Cologne-Ehrenfeld with raw red rubble aggregate.

These familiar materials are used in no customary structural way. Ordinary brick walls compose

125
Cologne-Stadtgarten.
St. Alban's.
Hans Schilling

124
Hanover-Linden.
Martinskirche.
Dieter Oesterlen

the principal structure of church and tower at Schwarz's St. Andreas church in Essen and, capped by a conical roof, of Gottfried Böhm's 126 graceless circular St. Theresia's in Cologne-Mulheim. They served Goebel well in his simple gable-roofed St. Albertus-Magnus, also in Essen. Bartning needed only brick walls together with ordinary wood roof trusses or laminated wood girders and bents to produce most of his moving Notkirchen in 1951. Wooden roofs are seldom complicated, though something is made of the converging geometry of bents in the rounded apses of churches such as Bartning's Luther-Notkirche, and simple wooden ceilings are employed with fine 61 effect in Baumgarten's Kirche am Lietzensee in Berlin. Brick is seldom used in more elaborate ways such as the brick longitudinal arches of 127 Dominikus Böhm's St. Engelbert at Cologne-Riehl, and even this was built in 1930–1932 when such backward-looking exercises were still regarded as commendable.

Metal structures do not appear often, but they are interesting when they do. Joachim Schür-128 mann's St. Pius in Cologne-Flittard has slender posts which strive upward to hold a three-dimensional steel framework supporting the roof and hanging walls. Rudolf Schwarz made an imaginative combination when he supplied a new altar area for the still remaining nave of a three-129 aisled neo-Gothic church, the Liebfrauen at Cologne-Mülheim. A three-part saddle roof over this area is supported by interesting three-dimensional tubular trusses resting sometimes on the old walls and twice on free-standing rectangular columns which set off the altar. The triangular motif is reflected in the narrow high windows paired at the valleys.

As everywhere else these days, concrete offers the widest range of forms but never to the plastic extent sometimes achieved in France, Brazil, or America. Indeed, it has been used with great dignity and restraint in Germany. The Böhms' 130 St. Anna's is clearly one of the most graceful. Delicate columns, tapering downward, support graceful ribs which also taper toward the crown or the tips of the cantilevers. These in turn support a palpably thin ceiling of exposed concrete. At 131 St. Joseph's in Cologne-Braunsfeld, Schwarz used a set of transversely ridged concrete roofs supported on concrete columns and repeated the gable ribs lower down in mirror image to frame large 132 lozenge-shaped windows. In his St. Mechtern's Church at Cologne-Ehrenfeld, six simple square concrete pillars support a flat slab roof. In the 133 equally direct St. Christophorus in Cologne-Riehl, he used a long-span, high, slender, concrete rectangular frame and joists. A similar concrete column and flat arch forms Hesse and Schulze's Lukaskirche at Cologne-Flittard. There are some more complicated forms: the parabolic ribs of St. Rochus which Schneider-Esleben now regrets; the interesting parabolic pumice concrete ribs of St. Engelbert's; the heavily triangulated free-standing concrete bents, exterior to the wall, of Fritz Kreidt's Evangelische Gnadenkirche in Essen-Altstadt; the more informal, even rural, 134 forms of Schädel's St. Joseph's Church in Hasloch am Main; the beginnings of brutalism 43 at the Regina Martyrium in Berlin; the eccentric St. Canisius by Reinhard Hofbauer at the Berlin Interbau. More pleasing are the fully developed crisscross ribs of Werner Neumann's Weissfrauenkirche in Frankfurt and less so the scallops that fringe the porch of the same church. Finally, Baumgarten made a sensitive use of pleated 135 concrete at his Lietzensee Church, the folding of the roof descending to the ground at two points and everywhere corresponding to its gentle slope. There is therefore a wide range of concrete structure (though no wider than, if indeed so wide as,

126 left top
Cologne-Mülheim.
St. Theresia's.
Gottfried Böhm

127 left bottom
Cologne-Riehl.
St. Engelbert's.
Dominikus Böhm

128 right top
Cologne-Flittard.
St. Pius.
Joachim Schürmann

129 right bottom
Cologne-Mülheim.
Liebfrauenkirche.
Rudolf Schwarz

130
Cologne-Ehrenfeld.
St. Anna's.
*Gottfried and Dominikus
Böhm*

131
Cologne-Braunsfeld.
St. Joseph's.
Rudolf Schwarz

132
Cologne-Ehrenfeld.
St. Mechtern's.
Rudolf Schwarz

133
Cologne-Riehl.
St. Christophus.
Rudolf Schwarz

134
Hasloch-am-Main.
St. Joseph's.
Hans Schädel

135
Berlin-Charlottenburg.
Church at Lietzensee.
Paul Baumgarten

136
Frankfurt-Bonames.
Notkirche.
Otto Bartning and others

137

Cologne-Braunsfeld.
Tower of St. Joseph's.

Rudolf Schwarz, V. Bernard

138

Unterrath. Evangelical
Church.

*Helmut Hentrich,
Hubert Petschnigg*

139

Düren. Christ Church.

*Helmut Hentrich,
Hans Heuser*

140

Berlin-Schöneberg. Tower
of Paul-Gerhardt Church.

*Hermann Fehling,
Daniel Gogel*

that known in the United States); and the shadow of Frederick Kiesler is nowhere to be seen.

The common factor in such diverse plans, materials, and structures and in the great variety of light arrangements and art I discussed previously seems to be that the interiors come first, that inside the churches one is most often aware of sincerity and simplicity of purpose, and only much later of the artifice of the architect. It is all summed up perhaps by the extraordinary and touching achievement of the Notkirchen of 1951, trying as Bartning said to "draw strength from the waste." Of these there are notable examples besides the Cologne church cited, such as the Dankeskirche 136 in Berlin-Wedding or the barnlike one in Frankfurt.

These churches, then, are simpler, more direct, more convincing and, though one hesitates to use the term, more sincere than most of their American contemporaries. They are also stronger, and that may be the significant difference.

The concern with the interior rather than the exterior is offset by the prominent bell towers that are either attached to or more usually stand free from the churches, in a country which likes the peal of bells on Sunday. A few of these towers are disastrous, such as the one applied later to Rudolf Schwarz's St. Michael's in Frankfurt. But a number of them are very fine from the simple brick shafts of St. Andreas, Essen, or St. Engelbert's, Cologne, to the elegant concrete shafts of 137 Allerheiligen, Frankfurt, and especially St. Joseph's, Cologne, or the Gnadenkirche in Essen. Schiffler's Evangelische-Kirche at Mannheim-Blumenau has a form reminiscent of Ronchamp. The greatest combination of height and slenderness has been achieved by Helmut Hentrich and 138 Hubert Petschnigg at the Evangelische-Kirche at 139 Unterrath and Hentrich and Hans Heuser at the Christuskirche in Düren.

Beside these, such later eccentricities as Fehling 140 and Gogel's tower at the Paul-Gerhardt-Kirche in Berlin-Schöneberg or Conrad Sage and Karl 4 Hebecker's steel atrocity at the Kirche Neu-Westend, also in Berlin, seem clumsy, self-conscious, and out of place if not positively antireligious. They are, fortunately, rare.

Why did the German work of this period surpass ours? We know that German churches had no more money to spend than our churches; we know that the Germans may have had some advantage because practically all their churches, Catholic or Evangelical, emphasize liturgy and are, therefore, at once more aware of and less suspicious of symbols. It is clear that more big-name German architects worked on churches than have done so here. Were American congregations wary of big names? Were big names not interested in doing low-cost churches at a loss to their offices, given the nature of American architectural practice? Would the results have been different? It is all part of one piece, I suspect, a mystical and speculative piece. I conclude that the Germans wanted churches more than we did, and so they got better ones just as they got better group housing, theaters, swimming baths, and parks, and we got better freeways, schools, and some office buildings. Perhaps great churches come about only when the religion is central and tough-thinking, more of "Ein Feste Burg" than "cool Siloam's Shady Rill."

This is not necessarily a stable situation in Germany. Everyone I talked to about it agreed that in the late forties and the fifties there had been a great surge of religious sentiment and that it was in these years that most of the best churches were built. They say that the spirit is dying away now and that the architects are more indulging in caprice. The little evidence I have confirms this view. Of my forty "best," four come from the decade of the thirties, four between 1945 and 1952, and then there are about four in each of the years 1953, 1954, 1955, 1956, 1957, and 1958, three in 1959 and 1960, and only three since. Moreover, the first eccentric church does not appear until 1953 while of the ten eccentrics, six are the product of the past three years.

The eccentricities can be very bad. Gottfried Böhm is, unhappily, more of an engineer than an artist, but he surpassed his generally clumsy achievements in St. Paulus at Velbert, produced with Fritz Hermes, which has a completely inappropriate combination of tower, a nave with a hanging roof, and a transept consisting of a large enveloping section of semicircular arch. Hofbauer's St. Canisius is to be criticized not only for its airplane-wing tower, which looks like the product of a body designer for General Motors, but for the strange wedged-shape plan, which does not coordinate well with an arched roof—this effect is somewhat less pleasant than the folding metal traveling cups we used to carry long ago. While Schiffler uses tough concrete with taste, Schädel does not; and Fritz Schaller's St. Johannes der Täufer in Leverkusen is an excellent example of how ugly and purposeless concrete design can become. No doubt the very worst of all these designers is Olaf Gulbrannsson, who combines ugly masonry in strange ways to produce most unpleasant evangelical churches such as the one at Schwebheim, near Schweinfurt or at Manching, near Ingolstadt.

A church, of course, has more important things to do than be pleasant, and as I said perhaps the great advantage of the German churches over the American is that they are less soft. Yet there is no achievement in being disagreeable as opposed to austere; and that is what, it seems to me, churches like the ones cited have managed to be. Their architects are probably not very good to start with, but even a good architect can do bad work if he forgets what the main purpose of his building is and admires architecture or himself perhaps more than he admires or even believes in God. This may, for example, be what is wrong with Aalto's new church in Wolfsburg which is much better than any of those just cited. Aalto is not an arrogant man and his taste is fairly sure. But the structure in Wolfsburg leaves an impression of somewhat too much architecture and somewhat too little church. On this and other similar evidence, it does look as though the great decade of German church building has come to an end. But it has left a notable legacy and it demonstrates again Eliel Saarinen's statement that people get the architecture they deserve, if we agree that you will deserve good architecture of any type when your heart wants it very much—and not otherwise.

It should be an unsettling experience for a young American soldier who returns from worshiping in Karl Mertz's multifaith American church in Berlin-Dahlem to what he is likely to find with few exceptions in his local parish. The Air Force Academy Chapel in Colorado Springs was a dedicated and serious experiment by a serious and able architect. Despite its prizes, it seems to me to have partly failed precisely because what was to be done inside it lacked the clarity, even the sincerity, of purpose to be found in the great churches from St. Vitale to the Notkirchen. What happens in a church at a military academy is of course determined by a colonel-chaplain and not by an architect. It is stupid to criticize Sir Basil Spence for not having reformed the Anglican church in the process of designing Coventry Cathedral. If Belluschi's churches are soft and Schwarz's or Striffler's are strong, it is because one congregation chose the church of comfort and the other the church militant or accepted architectural suggestions of that choice. Good religious work is impossible to compromisers. If the symbols of religion are faint in one country and strong in another, it is a little too easy to dismiss the country with the symbols as superstitious. When the social rooms of the church outweigh the baptisteries and the sanctuaries, the architecture will inevitably be different—and less moving.

141
Berlin-Dahlem. American Church.
Karl Mertz

Among the German commercial buildings there are a handful of fine design. They do not by any means outshine many of the great American accomplishments such as Lever House and Seagram's in New York, the newer Continental Casualty and Assurance Company Building in Chicago, or such partially successful experiments as the Sunset-Vine Tower in Hollywood for the Los Angeles Federal Savings and Loan, or even Marina City in Chicago. On the other hand, they reveal no such monstrous desecrations of the cityscape as Pan American in New York or Prudential in Boston.

There is something to be said for a populous, thriving, modern, commercial-industrial country which has not found it necessary to express anybody's greed or egotism in more than twenty-six stories, the number boasted by the highest building in Germany, the BASF by Hentrich and Petschnigg in Ludwigshafen. The next highest is the Phoenix-Rheinrohr (Thyssen) building in Düsseldorf at twenty-four stories, by the same architects. The highest building in Berlin is Schwebes and Schossberger's edifice erected in 1959–1960 for Telefunken. It is twenty-one or twenty-two stories and about 270 feet.

There is a great deal to be said for how these buildings are sited; they have not defeated the general urban landscape as the Hilton has in London, the Prudential has in Boston and Chicago, and the two proposed monsters by Yamasaki may do in New York. It needs to be learned that there are relations of scale which are so bad that no excellence of individual design can overcome them. New urban scales are inevitable, but there is an agreeable rate of change and a disagreeable one. These lessons seem to be better understood or, for whatever reason, better heeded in Germany. The Mannesmann in Düsseldorf graces the river,

the Phoenix-Rheinrohr profits from the adjacent city parks but augments them, too, with its own grace, and the Telefunken in Berlin is a component and not a domineering element on the Ernst Reuter Platz.

There is something to be said too for single ownership by a serious corporation as is usual in Germany, in contrast to the inflated, realtor-gamesmanship practiced by the notorious urban promoters of America (they exist in many places; they are at their worst in New York only because New York does both its best and its worst at the scale of the behemoth). Among other things, separate ownership tends to restrict giantism. Lufthansa could not afford to build the Pan American Building in New York (neither probably could Pan American). Single ownership and tenancy also permit a more open planning. Reception and guardianship can be exercised (and are) in the foyer so there is much less use of upstairs space for reception and much less unnecessary charging up and down in elevators (the elevators, by the way, are Swiss, and excellent).

It is surprising and pleasing to note the decency and modesty of commercial furnishings. It is surprising because of our image of German pomposity and its need for hierarchy and status symbols. The differences between general floors and executive suites are muted in most of the buildings, perhaps only for the present and as a consequence of the bad repute some of the big companies had to live down at the end of the Nazi era.

The number of people who have to have private offices seems to be much fewer. The idea that the corporate image can be enhanced by the ownership of Barcelona chairs just because they are expensive seems to have escaped the German tycoons and their architects. Their cliché, a refreshing substitute for the Barcelona chair, is to

142
Ludwigshafen. BASF
skyscraper.
Helmut Hentrich,
Hubert Petschnigg

143
Ludwigshafen. BASF
skyscraper, lobby.
*Helmut Hentrich,
Hubert Petschnigg*

144
Cologne. Broadcasting
House. Lobby.
P. F. Schneider

have an abundance of plants everywhere, even in preposterous places (as we would look at it), and other plants than philodendrons. It seems to me a more attractive cliché, and tending the foliage as good a way to waste secretarial time as a coffee break.

But except for the urban arrangements, these are modest differences and they do not suggest that German office buildings are better than ours. Nor are they, I think, worse.

The fundamental plans, of course, resemble ours in the principle that off the ground floor the various levels will have the same generally undifferentiated office space, elevators, toilets, and so on. The use of the space is somewhat different from ours, but as this is an expression of the differences in how German and American managers work at their daily tasks, it is not likely to change very much in either country in a great hurry. The lobbies tend to be less public, less designed to impress, though certainly pleasant enough at a rather quiet, domestic scale. Hentrich and Petschnigg's lobby for the administration buildings of the Rheinhausen foundry or the same firm's lobby in the

143 BASF skyscraper are about as elaborate as they get. But they do gain charm not only from plants but from the ability to use open stairs of which they take full advantage, as, for example, in Hermkes, Sanders, and Zess' Provincial Banking and Accounting Head Office in Kiel, Peter

144 Schneider's lobby for the Broadcasting House in Cologne, and Max Meid and Helmut Romelick's entrance hall for the sales offices of Farbwerke Hoechst Company in Frankfurt. Thanks to American safety laws, the escalator, and American architectural approaches, we have almost forgotten here what a splendid element of architectural amenity a great interior stair may be, at least for a nation which can walk without puffing. (Philip Johnson did achieve it in the Kline Laboratories at Yale.)

Most of the good German buildings are so small that they would hardly attract attention here at 145 all. Characteristic are Paul Baumgarten's Ruhrkohle in Berlin. Bernhard Pfau's house for the glass industry in Düsseldorf, Godber Nissen's administration building for the Reemtsma Company in Hamburg, and Oesterlen's administration 146 building of the Ilseder foundry at Peine, which has fine architectural details.

A number of these buildings reveal the same trend toward acceptance of Miesian solutions that was evident here a few years ago. Apparently, once the idea was fixed, the Germans needed no American tutelage to follow Mies as faithfully as we do. One has only to compare the American consulate at Frankfurt-am-Main, as good a building as there is in town, with Oesterlen's building at Peine or Hermann Wunderlich's and Reinhold 147 Klüser's central administration of the Cologne Kaufhof store to see that Skidmore, Owings, and Merrill had little to teach the Germans, at least at that moment. The best commercial building in Germany in the Miesian vein is Schneider-Esleben 148 and Knothe's addition to Peter Behrens' old Mannesmann Building in Düsseldorf; the best Miesian building in Germany may be the Stuttgart parliament.

There are other high buildings, if not skyscrapers, which the Germans like to show you. An imposing one in a manner which I think has happily faded away is Dierschke and Zinsser's 149 Continental House in Hanover, now more than ten years old. Albricht Lange and Hans Mitzlaff's insurance building in Mannheim, built some six years later, is transitional but straightforward, pleasant, and convincing. More stylish with the architects and no doubt more perfect in detail are 150 Egon Eiermann's office building for Steinkohlenbergwerke in Essen, completed in 1960, which despite his high repute I find unnecessarily somber,

145
Berlin. Ruhrkohle building.
Paul G. R. Baumgarten

146
Peine. Ilseder Foundry.
Administration building.
Dieter Oesterlen

147 left
Cologne. Kaufhof central
administration building.
Hermann Wunderlich,
Reinhold Klüser

148 right
Düsseldorf. Mannesmann
skyscraper.
Schneider-Esleben, Knothe

149
Hanover. Continental
rubber factory.
Administration building.
Dierschke, Zinsser

150
Essen. Essen coal mine.
Administration building.
Egon Eierman

151 left
Berlin. IBM administration building.
Rolf Gutbrod

152 right
Essen.
Rheinisch-Westfälisches
Electric works (RWE).
Headquarters.
Professor Dustmann

and Rolf Gutbrod and Bernhard Binder's still
151 later building for IBM in Berlin, which is much
praised but which, like most of Gutbrod's work,
seems to me unnecessarily tricky, this time at the
spandrels and on the end wall. A building which is
rising now in Essen and whose main slab at least
seems elegant is Dustmann's design for the
152 Rheinisch-Westfälisches Elektrizitätswerke.

Of all the German high buildings, I found
153 Hentrich and Petschnigg's Phoenix-Rheinrohr or
Thyssen Building in Düsseldorf the most ingratiating. It is beautifully located both on the present
landscape and on what is planned. It towers above
Düsseldorf, but it does not smash the scale of the
city. Its three thin slabs arise from function (as
the other thin German buildings do), that is, the
legal limitation on how far an office dweller can be
from a window, but this is translated imaginatively
into the sandwich that has emerged. The con-
nection of the slabs with huge steel bracing
trusses such that they become a significant element
of the visible design is brilliant. The interior spaces
are fine, and the building is handsome from almost
every point of view, more from the ends or
obliquely than head on, to be sure. It seems to me
to be one of the truly handsome undoctrinaire high
buildings of our day, to be compared with Gio
Ponti's Pirelli Building in Milan or Seagram's in
New York, and really surpassing Seagram's in its
important and happy effect on its local urban landscape.

There are those who differ. They compare it
148 unfavorably with Schneider-Esleben's Mannesmann Building in the same town. Some do this
because they can endure nothing but straight Mies,
and to them we need pay scant attention. But there
are many, including the architects of the Phoenix
itself, who praise the Mannesmann and its architect
for the perfection of the details and deplore the
Phoenix because some details are sloppy. Both the

praise and the blame are justified. It is the conclusion which is uncertain. One wonders how many
users and admirers of a building ever see the sloppy
or even "dishonest" details before some erudite
critic points them out. There is, after all, the
evidence of St. Sofia, the painted joints of the
North German naves, the false fronts of the baroque, and the carelessly put together master-
pieces of Le Corbusier. There can be no argument
that perfection of detail improves the life and
performance of a building. When the perfection of
detail becomes a matter of style, then the question
arises, who is looking? For the good life of a
civilization, peoples' architects are more important
than architects' architects. If the only people an
architect can impress are himself and a few other
architects and some critics and magazine editors,
architecture will become either extravagant or dry.
Ideally, of course, we would have handsome forms
and fine detail in one perfectly crafted package.
But it may be (and it seems so from both literary
and art history) that those who labor most skillfully and patiently to provide the perfection of
detail are rarely if ever those who can produce the
ultimately and immediately stunning whole. It
is a most difficult question, but it is answerable to
me in a simple way. The City of Düsseldorf has a
fine aesthetic conflict to ponder over the years in
the presence of two of the finest office buildings
in Germany. I will wager that the question will
not be discussed save in the most effete of critical
circles.

153
Düsseldorf.
Phoenix-Rheinrohr A.G.
''Das Thyssenhaus.''
Helmut Hentrich,
Herbert Petschnigg

Government Buildings

Not many genuinely fine large governmental buildings have been built in the world between the Houses of Parliament in London and Chandigarh or Brasília. In this time, dictators, right and left, have had generally reactionary taste and bad at that, while in the democracies men have not been elected to high office for their good taste and high aesthetic aspirations. Winston Churchill, Franklin Roosevelt, and Dwight Eisenhower did not add much to the aesthetic dignity of their countries, though each of them "knew what he liked." John F. Kennedy's heart was on the right side, but his taste and that of his closest advisers seemed to lean a little to the prettier moderns, which is better, no doubt, than if it had leaned to the architecture of the National Gallery or the new Smithsonian. I have not examined any architectural debates that may have taken place on the floor of the parliaments of Delhi or Bonn, if indeed there were any, but it is certain that whatever their merits Nehru was no Akbar, or Adenauer a mad Ludwig. No one asks or knows what Erhard or Brandt thinks or cares about architecture—or Lyndon Johnson. It is perhaps just as well. The national architectural standard will not arise as a qualifying or disqualifying argument at any national convention, and it is not part of the examination for any civil service posts. Taste in design of postage stamps is not one of the qualifications for Postmaster General, or taste in buildings, for the Secretaries of State, Treasury, Commerce, Interior, or Defense, all of whom control the approval of a great many important buildings. Our public architectural debates, when they happen (which is not often enough) are as silly as those which surrounded the discussion in our Congress of the Air Force Academy Chapel. Here it was considered significant that a Senator thought the design sacrilegious and that President Eisenhower blushed his characteristic angry red when he learned that the design was not "a joke." The President's taste was little different from Chairman Khrushchev's, though backed by less power. The chapel was neither sacrilegious nor a joke, whatever else it was, and it survived the national display of ineptitude in the arts, but not without losing its trees.

I do not know whether debates on architecture occur in the Bundestag, but I do know that there are almost no interesting buildings at the federal level in Germany just as there are almost none here. (Perhaps for political reasons, which in this case transcend aesthetic reasons, the height of dreary sobriety is reached in Bonn where not even the Bundestag is really interesting. Exceptions to this are sometimes to be noted when our government builds embassies abroad; and curiously enough the Germans too have built better federal architecture outside their own country. A noteworthy example of this is Egon Eiermann's Chancery for the Federal Republic of Germany in Washington, D. C. Eiermann's high repute for sensitive proportion and meticulous detail is even more obviously warranted by the chancellery, whose graceful and humane simplicity and quiet attention to the terrain make it not only his best work but the best building to have been built in our National Capital in a long time.

There is naturally more variety at the state level with a considerable difference in what is possible in reactionary and bourgeois Bavaria than what might happen in Lower Saxony. I have already expressed my opinion on the romantically reconstructed Rathaüser and the eclectic town hall in Stuttgart. Typical examples of the dull bureaucratic style are to be found all over Germany, such as Prendel's Public Assistance Office in Hanover or the Revenue Office in Augsburg. Modest exceptions to the rule can be found here and there, such as the Federal Criminal Investigation Building in Wiesbaden, the Fiscal Administration Building in Frankfurt, or the Ministry of Economics in Stuttgart. I have already written about a partially notable exception in Oesterlen's rebuilding and addition to the Lower Saxony Representative Assembly Hall in Hanover.

The outstanding and almost isolated example of this type is to be found in the parliament of Baden-Württemberg, built in Stuttgart in 1960–1961 by Viertel, Linde, and Heinle. Under the far from occasional pelts of rain the Landtagsgebäude looks almost as dark as Seagram's does on a sunny day. This is one of the most distinguished buildings in Germany, very Miesian, magnificently equipped in the offices of the various Members of Parliament. In some ways it is a child's toy with its automatic Venetian-blind lifters, its local temperature control, its concealed private wash-basins. There is an elegant plenary hall, a brilliant lower public foyer, and stairs with the attractive wall made of large fossil-bearing stones from Holzmaden mentioned earlier, sculpture by Marini, paintings by Schlemmer, and so on. This building has real distinction and elegance. But the legislators give it dignity, too. Boston is building a distinguished modern city hall. How it will look after a few years will depend as much upon the City Council and its hangers-on as upon the architecture. The great General Court of Massachusetts has not always ennobled the Bulfinch capitol.

Except for housing where municipal standards are determining and where ideological "sobriety" or economy are not applied, the general governmental score in Germany, then, seems not too different from ours—not high enough. But there is one group of public buildings from which we could learn. These occur at one of the points where government meets the public face to face and in a personal way, that is in the post offices.

154
Stuttgart. Parliament of
Baden-Württemberg.
Viertel, Linde, Heinle

155
Waldshut/Oberrheim.
Post Office.
Hans Merkenthaler

156
Mannheim. Post Office.
Friedrich Bauer

The design rests in state rather than federal hands, and it is hard to find an unpleasant post office in Germany even in big cities. In small-town America the local postmaster is usually friendly even if his pens will not write and his typewriter is obsolete. In Arlington, Massachusetts, there are even plants in one of the branch post offices, but at the expense of the postmaster and not the U.S.A., which cannot afford any such nonsense. In our metropolitan post offices obviously there are no plants. There are plants in all the post offices of Germany, and they are not procured at the cost of the local official. But then mailing a letter is a more serious thing in Germany than it is here—and more fun, too—just as most foreign stamps are.

The post offices vary in architectural style from region to region, and they are different in the country than in the city. In villages and small towns and even in suburbs they are generally domestic, even residential, or deliberately quaint in style as though everyone were living in a German Williamsburg or in old Forest Hills Gardens on Long Island. Typical are the units at Dortmund-Eving or Bochum-Weine where only the sign POST distinguishes them from the houses. This attitude of conformity to the surroundings no doubt explains the historicism of the Postamt at Lübeck.

In the larger cities, though, the buildings are among the more distinguished in town, centrally located, friendly but not pompous. The public rooms are usually pleasant places to do business— spacious without being oppressively monumental, well lighted, full of plants, thoughtfully planned for customer convenience of every kind. Part of the ground space is often leased to commercial shopping arcades which liven the whole area. The post offices offer a startling contrast to ours, which, however, improved, still forcefully recall the corroded gummy inkwells of our childhood. One can cite any number of examples at Wolfsburg, at

155 Waldshut, at Dortmund, and so on. Wolf Stubler's hall in the central post office of Stuttgart has distinction. The head post office in the Parade-156 platz in Mannheim, designed by Friedrich Bauer, is among the best. The old dignified, even pretentious, building with its bad sandstone façade in Italian Renaissance style was burned out in the war and properly regarded as quite unsuitable for restoration. The new building in an equally prominent position has a pleasant façade, an ingratiating entrance, a foyer running through the building from street to street with shop displays on one side, inviting counters, well-designed mailboxes, phone booths, a casino, and a wonderfully named "Windfang fur Briefannahme." The entire impression is that the post office department wants your goodwill just as though it had a competitor. Perhaps the United States might some day have a nonpolitical Postmaster General? Perhaps it would not matter. The budget has to be balanced somewhere, and where better than in corroded inkwells, dingy federal architecture, and poor stamp design?

Postscript

There are a few other buildings in Germany which should be cited more to complete the record than because they offer provocative suggestions.

It was a pleasure, for example, to see how convenient (and common) it was to go to art galleries where the temporary exhibitions are everywhere displayed with fine taste and where the permanent collections of near-contemporary work are much better than one imagined could possibly have survived the Nazi purges of "decadent" art. But with few exceptions the galleries themselves cannot teach us much.

The best gallery is, no doubt, the modest museum Folkwang in Essen, which has fine circulation and light, and generously cooperating 157 patios. Another fine building is Werner Düttmann's Academy of Arts in Berlin, which serves both as a gallery especially well adapted for three-dimensional display and as a club for visiting academicians of the arts. Perhaps the forthcoming 158 Berlin Gallery of the Twentieth Century to be built by Mies near the Philharmonic will also merit an accolade if the great areas of glass do not spoil everything but sculpture.

What these buildings do suggest is that their architects have consistently built to display art rather than architecture, and in that sense the works are quieter than well-known galleries by Wright in New York or Rudolph in Wellesley. If in a church you cannot concentrate on the Eucharist because the architect has been so impressive, something is probably wrong. The point is equally valid for a theater or an art gallery, as Kahn and Johnson, for example, have perceived.

The schools do not on the whole require much pause. Based on a more austere theory of education, they will seem inflexible to Americans and not very gay. Since swimming and other communal recreational facilities are provided in other types of excellent communal buildings, and since schools

157
Berlin. Academy of Arts.
*Werner Düttmann,
Sabine Schumann*

157a
Aerial view.

157b
Theater.

158
Berlin. Gallery of the
Twentieth Century. Model.
Ludwig Mies van der Rohe

159
Hanover. Wilhelm-Busch
School.
Dieter Oesterlen

161
Hirschau. Kindergarten,
Amberger Kaolin Factory.
Hans and Trudi Maurer

160
Munich-Dornfinkenweg.
Municipal kindergarten.
Hans and Trudi Maurer

are seldom expected to serve, for example, as parental community halls, the school complexes will seem uninteresting to most American visitors. The play and leisure courts, too, are usually functional and bare, with little of what the late Dorothy Thompson used to denounce, wrongly, as extravagant nonsense. Kindergartens on the other hand will often look well enough to justify their charming name.

A few schools a visitor might try to see are Scharoun's Geschwisterschule in Lünen; Oester-159 len's Wilhelm-Busch-Schule in Hanover, which is one of the best *gymnasiums;* Harold Leonhardt's Goetheschule, also in Hanover, a good technical school; the moderately charming Silcher-Volks-schule in Stuttgart-Zuffenhausen by Günter Wilhelm and Karl Häge and the Gartenbauamt of the City of Stuttgart; and Friedrich Kraemer's Abendschule in Dortmund, one of the purest of the formal types. American pavilion types can be found in Germany, for instance Otto Apel's school in Bad Godesberg, but neither the German weather nor the German view of education seem to call for California types on the Rhine.

There are, on the other hand, a good many attractive lower schools. Examples are Peter Poelzig's Markt-Schule in Oberhausen and Paul Seitz's school at Leverkusen-Manfort. Herta Hammerbacher laid out the grounds for both of these. There is Walter Hämer's Kindertagesstätte in Hanover-Bothfeld, and the work of Hans and 160 Trudi Maurer at the municipal kindergarten in Munich or the works kindergarten at the Amberger 161 Kaolin-Werke in Hirschau.

Of German university architecture there is even less to be said now that American colleges and universities are rioting in architecture from coast to coast. If they are losing cohesion and even repose thereby, it seems better than that they should have remained as dull, even dreary, as they often were

and as certainly the German universities largely are, especially those being rebuilt on the classic foundations where most of the modern work, when permitted, is timid and unconvincing. There are some exceptions. For example, some of the 162 German student housing in Berlin's Siegmunds Hof, designed by Klaus H. Ernst, is interesting, but more for the suggestion it makes about another way of providing student domiciles than for architecture. The new library for the Friedrich-Wilhelm University at Bonn is not bad and seems refreshing in Germany. Yet it would scarcely be noticed here. On the other hand, the most one would care to say of the buildings at the Free University at Dahlem is that they are competent and decent.

The revived Technische Hochschulen did seem to me to have more spirit and probably not only in their architecture. But the buildings remain severely functional, well-expressed places to work. When they become architecturally exciting, it is generally because the activity inside requires unusual architectural forms as, for example, a towing tank might. It is this which accounts, I think, for most of the interest at Darmstadt in the lecturehall and experiment station for hydraulic structures and foundation construction, or in the best buildings at Aachen. Paul Seitz's Hochhaus and Auditorium Maximum at Hamburg have modest competence, but there are better examples of both elsewhere in the world. There is some excitement and promise in the new buildings Rolf Gutbrod is putting up at Stuttgart, but they remain mostly quite literal. The most elegant, because the designers are men of refinement, are those built at Brunswick, rising beside nineteenth-century wreckage but with much more conviction than in a comparable situation at Berlin-163 Charlottenburg. There is Oesterlen's Obertrakt-Hochhaus and, the most polished of any university

162
Berlin-Tiergarten.
Siegmunds Hof student
housing.
Klaus H. Ernst

163
Brunswick. Technical High
School. Multistory building.
Dieter Oesterlen

164
Brunswick. Technical High
School. Auditorium.
F. W. Kraemer

buildings I saw, Friedrich W. Kraemer's auditorium and faculty offices with a library to come. The plan of the library seems to me overly complicated and the idea of tucking a few scholars aloof in the tower a little strange, but this may work. The auditorium is unusual in that its two side walls are glass, so there is a lot of natural light when wanted; but it can be completely closed in, and quickly, by an elaborate system of mechanically operated shades. A few of these buildings would look well on any American campus but would cause little comment, and the most brilliant of them make almost no effort at display.

For variety, titillation, brilliance, and nonsense, even for decadence, you will have to look on the campuses of America where architects are seldom professors but seem to know what professors ought to like. I do not mean this to sound surly about American collegiate architecture, which is the most imaginative and exciting in the world. This is true despite its excesses and its mediocrities. And I am sure it is because the professors have had little to do with it. It has faltered only when trustees who are little wiser than professors in aesthetic matters have thought they were. With all their faults, the bad things at New Haven are infinitely superior in their final effect to the dreary compromises in Cambridge, England, or the pedestrian workhouses at Berlin-Charlottenburg. And it is better for the future to have the bad examples if they are serious and dramatic. The unhappy building for Architecture and the Fine Arts at Yale may serve to prevent worse ones later; the success of Saarinen at the University of Chicago Law School may encourage others to know that neither Gothicists nor librarians are always right.

To close this categorical survey of building architecture with a glance at German factories, it is my impression that they are no longer as exciting as in the days when Behrens and Gropius asserted that they were or could be important architectural monuments. It is a little easier to take their dullness for granted now. Heavy-industry buildings remain heavy-industry buildings. They continue to photograph very well, especially in the early morning or late evening when the strongly shadowing light and the impressionistic smoke act both to reveal and to conceal their powerful masses and musculature. Inside, they are something else again.

The Cities

In the end, all the planning and the rebuilding has to respond to a simple collective question—how happy is the total result? Despite the excellences, or the mediocrities, or the vagaries of the new German architecture, it is at the city level that any new architectural phoenix must be measured.

THE PLANNERS

Modern German planners started with very considerable legacies. The people were used to the idea that cities owned woods nearby in which one could and did tramp and picnic, free and safe. They were used to princely parks in the city, such as the Schlossgarten and the Parksee in Stuttgart, or nearby, such as the Nymphenburg of Munich. They had experienced princely plans such as those of Karlsruhe and imperial plans such as those of Berlin. They had large industrial legacies such as the Villa Hügel and the Waldtheater which the Krupps dedicated to Essen. They had important commercial legacies such as those of the Hansa towns, and the fruits of urban foresight such as the horticultural park Planten un Blomen in Hamburg. They were a people who loved trees and silviculture, which they practiced with skill and affectionate understanding, and flowers which they used with pleasure and restraint. Where else, for example, save perhaps in Finland, could one find a memorial statue to a forester in the center of a big city? Thus they need no lessons in public greenbelting and have been resistant to lopping off an acre of park here and there to make a school or a highway as is done so consistently in New York or Boston without any very loud and certainly no effective opposition. They are quite prepared to defend and even to augment the extensive existing greenbelts and accept the new federal and state plans for land consolidation and maintenance, even in rural areas. These, combined with the generally noble German traditions of land use, seem to assure the preservation of German countryside and the German cityscape against some of the depredations we have witnessed here.

So Germans have been used for a long time to a considerable state control of land and to serious restrictions on uninhibited private exploitation and development. Until the people of the United States understand that these are not slippery roads to the perdition of "socialism," beautiful and happy cities will become more and more difficult to make in America, or to preserve. Some time ago President Johnson proposed fairly modest federal provisions to assist in large land acquisitions as opposed to the piecemeal private development that produces slurbs, not communities. Even these were referred to by Miami homebuilders as federal "boondoggles" likely to become "ghost communities."

Long before the war, almost every German city had a wide array of cultural activities and buildings to house them, usually blessed with substantial support by city and state. The German city dwellers were without exception used to enjoying fine zoos, botanical gardens, swimming baths, and other playgrounds, plus a rich array of theaters, halls, and art galleries. They knew how to use them and used them a lot. They wanted them in the new cities, too; and appropriations for the arts could be taken for granted, not as something to be fought for and yielded grudgingly.

They were accustomed to group housing and therefore to concentrated cities, to the use of public transportation which was kept in fine repair, to walking even in the rain, to bicycles, to shopping in specialty shops rather than in mass markets, to the daily walk to the bakery for fine, heavy, fresh bread, to concerts in the open air, to street decorations, and to quiet at night, even in the cities, so that Joseph von Eichendorff could speak of how "the fountains sleepily murmur all through the splendorous summer night."[13]

They were used to planning, too. All the cities had plans; Berlin in particular, had an elaborate one. By 1913 there was official approval of building plans in Berlin by which

had they ever been executed, approximately 21 million people could eventually have lived in the city area. But in 1925 the city officials decided to release only 193 of the city's 340 square miles for building purposes and to keep the rest permanently green. The parks, woods and lakes … reaches far into the city. … .[14]

They knew how to use their great rivers for commerce and manufacture, to be sure, for these were and still are major arteries; but they also knew how to preserve parts of the river for beauty and recreation—even in the close, huddled cities of the Ruhr.

They had intense local city pride and rivalry, more deep-seated than that between the states whose boundaries had shifted so often. This was an asset when it came to building a finer separate city and a liability when it came to interurban cooperation. It still is. The chief cities of the Ruhr have each about 600,000 people and there are a number of others, all essentially contiguous, running around 200,000 to 300,000 population. The total population of this metropolitan area, connected by autobahn and now also by a new Ruhr Schnellweg and by an efficient network of rails, comes to millions. Yet almost every urban unit has its own opera, its own city theater, its own gallery, so that there must be a dozen rival opera houses; and one would not be likely to go from Gelsenkirchen to Düsseldorf to the opera though this would be easier than going to Lincoln Center from

[13] That was some time ago. Try sleeping now on a main street of Trier or Stuttgart!

[14] Wolf Schneider, *Babylon Is Everywhere* (New York: McGraw-Hill, 1963), p. 261.

many parts of New York City. I suspect there is more good than harm in this. The Metropolitan might even be better, though less smug and less expensive, if it had competition from Newark, Jersey City, Brooklyn, the Bronx, and Yonkers.

The planners have had some disadvantages, too. Though accustomed to planning, the people are a little tired of being managed, and resistant to new bureaucratic orders. So a good deal of persuasion has been needed. In situations where the urban land is still in private hands, it is not quite so easy to take it by procedures of eminent domain in order, for example, to rearrange streets or to rectify boundaries, and very often the solution has been one of trading rather than of expropriation.

HANOVER

The Hanover plan is highly regarded by Germans who know it. Its maker, Rudolf Hillebrecht, has the highest national and international reputation of any of the German planners. But Hanover is a city in transition and suffering from the discomforts of transition. Years from now, it may be a fine city if the plans are carried out. Today it is a confusing, even a confused, and not altogether delightful city. Since I am trying here to deal with the German present and not the German future, I shall not dwell on the forward aspects of the plan.

Here let me cite only one important concept of Professor Hillebrecht's, which many praise or profess but which few practice: "It is not the business house that counts, but the business street, not the modern industrial building, but situation and set-up of the whole industrial quarter; not the apartment house, but the residential quarter; not the administrative building, but the governmental quarter; not the Lower Saxony Stadium, but the sporting area; not the school itself, but the school center; not the restored historical building, but the whole 'Isle of Tradition.'" This is the most important aesthetic principle behind planning, and it ought to govern rebuilding, redevelopment, and expansion everywhere; but it is extremely hard to achieve. Where the government controls an entire area, the principle may be followed, but the bureaucratic details may be too dull. In our country at least, private controlling institutions such as universities or the Rockefeller Center Corporation have been unable to control themselves; and where the land ownership is multiple, the egotism of individual architects and the competitive urge of individual clients has offered a sure invitation to chaos. Yet censoring commissions are unpopular and have usually, like the one in Washington, acted as brakes to progress while not being very effective in preventing ugly changes. This is a problem we must solve if our cities are to be pleasant. It is good to find a city where the program is at least categorically stated. I know of no such complete program for New York, or San Francisco, or Boston; and it does not seem to matter much whether the director of redevelopment has affection for urban beauty as in Philadelphia or San Francisco or is indifferent to, even scornful of, it as in Boston or New York.

The Hanover planners, like those of West Berlin, well know that keeping the public aware of what they hope to achieve is the best way in the end of achieving it. I have already mentioned the four models of Hanover in the Town Hall.

This use of large models to inform the public of development plans, even to excite them about the future and to engage their criticism and their support, is widespread in Germany. It reaches its peak in West Berlin, where models are to be found in many parts of town and not just in official places which comparatively few may chance to visit. We certainly have seen its value in America in the temporary exhibition of the Golden Gate competition in San Francisco and on a permanent basis in Philadelphia; but not enough of our city planners seem to perceive the virtue of really trying to interest the citizenry, and many even think it safer to keep the public in the dark. Surely there is more to be gained than lost by interesting the public in competition proposals *before* the final judgments are rendered. This seems to be feared by American jurors and especially by professional advisers and consultants, who like to move in secret and then defend the winner with more or less vigor, depending on who is attacking it. It might be a good thing if the American public were occasionally more hysterical about what is being done to its cities, good and bad.

WEST BERLIN

The most promising features of German city planning are most evident in West Berlin. West Berlin is a special case in at least five respects. Nonetheless, it typifies, I think, what other German cities might aspire to, or come to, even under their different conditions.

The five differences, none of which is trivial, are:

1. *West Berlin has a physical wall* which is a reality and enforces completely defined boundaries. This has advantages and disadvantages for morale which move into other questions than those of planning. The boundaries have robbed the Berliners of most of their outlying parks and lakes, limiting such facilities, so much craved by all Germans, to the Tiergarten downtown and the city forests; Rüppel, Grünewald, Spandau, and Tegel, all to the west, embracing the Havel and Tegel lakes. These are excellent but totally inadequate, though much larger per capita than the green spaces in New York. Planning has got to find new green areas or other compensations to relieve the terrific weekend crowding of the two verdant facilities. The wall has the effect on the other hand of limiting the need for an automobile. Outside excursioning, motoring to other parts of Germany, and so on, are just too hard to arrange. The Untergrundbahn can reach the farthest local boundary easily. There is therefore no great reason for most West Berliners to own automobiles, or to use them regularly if they do. As a result the ownership ratio is lower than in most German cities, about 1 to 5 elsewhere and 1 to 7 in West Berlin, and the amount of intown driving is also reduced. But the wall has another benign effect, according to the planners. It prevents sprawl, but it also forces total planning. Not much of the valuable space can be left to accident; and the Berliners can

165

Berlin. Section from model
of city.

easily understand why this has to be so. Can a wall be made by either law or planned building? Some Chicago planners think so; I doubt it.

2. *West Berlin is a showcase,* and everybody knows it. The rest of Germany likes Berlin almost for the first time and is proud of it. It is accepted that West Berlin should have more than a proportional share of federal support; it has also attracted an unusual amount of private foreign funds.

The Congress Hall, the American Memorial Library, the Free University, the Academy of Arts, the English Gardens, and so on were fully paid for or materially assisted by foreign funds, largely American, largely private, and given to the city or one of its institutions. Corporations have had symbolic reasons for building fine offices there, especially international corporations. America's showcases up to now have been more private than federal.

3. *The imperial plan* endowed Berlin with broad avenues which can be used to serve major traffic flow even now. These avenues unhappily run into the wall and so can no longer provide a true network, and a new highway system must be developed. But it has a start in terms of wide streets which would be hard to find in most other cities of Germany, especially the many which reach back into the Middle Ages for their street layouts. We owe such imperial ways as we have to Dan Burnham and ought to stop scolding him.

4. *Berlin has a fine underground system.* (The elevated system used to be good, too, but it has deteriorated in equipment and is, I suspect, more useful in the eastern zone. Indeed, a ride on it makes you feel as though you were in the eastern zone.) In the subway, though, the cars are new and pleasant, the stations comfortable, even attractive, the interchanges easy. People are used to riding in it and continue to do so. This is not strange, for like the Paris Métro, the Moscow subway, and much of London's Underground, it is pleasant as New York's subway positively is not. As a consequence the planners can easily promote as much new subway as they can highways and be supported by the public. A truly integrated public and private transportation system is therefore possible. It might also be possible in New York if the various authorities were forced to give up their profitable autonomies and work together for the benefit of the whole city. Anyway, and fortunately for Berlin, it was impossible for a man to rise to power with as distorted a total view as is held by the abnormally efficient and energetic Robert Moses, who would be less destructive if he were less able. The powers of the Senator für Bau und Wohnungswesen in Berlin are just about right and well related to those of the other relevant ministers. Perhaps San Francisco will do as well—or Boston's new M.T.A.

5. *Berlin is still viewed as THE capital.* The theory is clear in most of official Germany whatever realists may mutter behind closed doors. It is that Bonn is transitory and that some day the capital will return to a united Berlin. This has the effect in Bonn of limiting the buildings of the Federal Republic to necessities, since glamorous, expensive official buildings there might imply that Bonn was becoming a permanent capital. Thus, as I have noted earlier, even the Bundestag of Bonn is rather dull and the ministries even more so. For these same reasons, foreign countries have not built impressive embassies and chancelleries in Bonn, far less, for example, than they have in New Delhi or than they might some day in New Berlin. The effect on Bonn is paralleled by effects on West Berlin. In the first place, the planners in West Berlin do in fact project their plans for the whole city, even though the work in the East has to be postponed. There is another most interesting result. One feature of the Berlin plan is a great cultural

avenue which is anchored at one end by the Tiergarten and the zoo and curves around until it reaches Hans Scharoun's new Philharmonic Hall, and the new museum by Mies, about to be built. Between these there will be an array of cultural buildings—about halfway completed, though there is a substantial undesignated area; and when you ask what this is for, you will be told with blue-eyed candor that it is reserved for embassies!

I suspect the powers of the planners and rebuilders of West Berlin are a little clearer than those in some of the other German cities, most of which have the confusion of hosting both city and state governments, unlike the Hansa cities where city and state governments coincide. So, although it seems that the Berlin accomplishments are the most interesting and promising, the conditions have no doubt been more favorable.

It need only be said further that the West Berlin program calls for clear and practical objectives, widely spaced residential quarters, modern business buildings, a broad traffic net, widened green areas, cultural avenues, and for recovering the functions of a capital. The planning law of August 1949, revised in 1956, provides for a land zoning plan covering village areas and areas for various uses: purely residential, generally residential, mixed, restricted industrial, purely industrial, and the center. It stipulates plot ratios corresponding to the building laws of the Federal Republic; and, of importance, it legally binds individual development plans. All this may seem routine enough until one sees how pleasant West Berlin is actually becoming and how much more pleasant it is likely to become; and this is because West Berlin cares about its housing, its parks, its recreational facilities, and especially about its museums, concert halls, and theaters—to all of which highways are usually expected to be obedient servitors.

THE OVER-ALL RESULT

In the end, of course, all this rebuilding and planning must meet this test:

Is my city really a pleasant one in which to live, after I have discounted my local pride and habit?

Is Boston's dirt tolerable to me simply because I have the Public Garden?

Is the dreary uniformity or the even deadlier efforts at diversity of all the hundreds of Cucamongas more than compensated for by the frequent sun?

It does become pretty subjective, of course. And it is hard for a passerby to know. In one sense, you can be objective since you are not involved in defending your own place against criticism. On the other hand, as a transient and a stranger, your opinions are bound to be colored by the happy and unhappy accidents of tourism, although you are not likely to conclude that Colmar would be a great place to live just because you had a noble lunch at the nearby Auberge de l'Ill and spent three fine hours in the old square and before the Grünewald Isenheim altar. Finally, however objective a person's judgment may seem, tastes differ. I liked Stuttgart; yet our young and intelligent German guide-driver was bored with it beyond measure and could hardly wait to escape from his home town—to Paris. Maybe I would be bored with Stuttgart in a fortnight.

Of course, there are not very many Parises—and maybe even Paris isn't any more. There are no Parises in Germany. But after Paris, if you want to find a pleasant city in France it will not be, save perhaps for Strasbourg, one of the big ones. If Germany lacks a Paris, it has many pleasant towns.

Planning has not made them all pleasant. Hamburg is delightful, as well as Stuttgart, Münster, and Düsseldorf (though many Germans in the Ruhr do not like Düsseldorf which they feel is dominated by nouveaux riches and snobs). Munich, which has done the least and is coasting on its history, is nonetheless often pleasant. Mannheim and Darmstadt have some good spots. There are delights, mostly ancient joys, in a number of smaller places like Bremen, Lübeck, Hildesheim, Limburg, to some extent Freiburg, and to a lesser extent Trier. And West Berlin is the most exciting of all though not feeling like a whole city.

There are many others which despite prodigious efforts and the best of intentions do not seem to be gaining ground as fine places. Brunswick and Hanover will probably make it, though at the moment they seem in great confusion. Cologne offers a mixed package, and in the suburbs a dreary package despite the many fine parish churches. Except for Düsseldorf (Essen may also be an exception because of enormous cultural efforts), most of the cities of the Ruhr—Dortmund, Duisburg, Gelsenkirchen, Geilenkirchen, Bochum, and so on—are really deadly. The pall of smoke still hangs over them—a repetition of the death cloud beneath an inversion layer remains possible —and though they can build a Schnellweg from Dortmund to Düsseldorf and beyond, they have not seen fit to emulate Pittsburgh and apply measures which are known to work in controlling smoke. Nuremberg is a sad reminder of its onetime charm. And Frankfurt-am-Main has nothing to redeem it so far as I could see except its world-famous zoo.

So the regeneration which I praise is an imperfect one. Moreover, it is hard to foresee whether the later developments will be forward or backward. Each of the cities I have mentioned, perhaps even Frankfurt, has one or more new buildings of considerable importance (Gelsenkirchen, for example, has its extraordinary theater); and yet many of them fail as total cities. This leads to the conviction that architecture is not enough. In view of how most architecture comes out, this is probably just as well. When I was in school, we were taught how to obscure the defects of our designs by rendering large black trees in front of them. It is a device scorned by the purists of today. But in it there was an element of truth which said that few buildings are so fine that they should stand stark and be protected from the incursions of trees. The only trouble is, it takes longer to grow a tree than to paint it in Chinese ink.

Without the trees or the Chinese ink, it is pretty clear that the most pleasant cities in Germany are the few medieval ones like Rothenburg which went untouched in the war and remain untouched by modern life. The next best are those which having suffered great damage are content to be new cities along new lines, the good examples being Berlin, Hamburg, Stuttgart, and Düsseldorf. Cities caught up in modern life but trying too hard to restore their past, like Hanover, or preserve it, like Munich, are having their troubles; and if they continue to be too sentimental and too short-sighted they may, like Frankfurt, become only ghastly reminders of another era.

But all of the German cities, the good and the bad, seem to me to be losing the main battle with the principal enemy of contemporary urbanity: the automobile.

It is not that the Germans are latecomers to the automobile. For a time they led the world in the development of superhighways. The Reichsautobahnen, constructed with military purposes primarily in mind, did indeed offer a fast highway system across much of the country; but the connections of the autobahnen into the central cores were primitive and narrow, and generally still are. The greatest difficulty of the German planners, like all others, has been to keep pace with the voracious automobile. They have generally not succeeded. Unless things improve greatly, German cities will in the end be degraded by the automobile as American cities have already been; and the fact that the Volkswagen is small will not be enough. The car is, of course, here to stay. But who is to be the servant? Berlin thus far, given its admittedly special circumstances, is the least subservient to the automobile.

But there are interesting things elsewhere which do not turn up in Berlin. Garages are better in Frankfurt, Cologne, Stuttgart. Essen has an interesting protected footwalk system with clear pedestrian lines. Both Essen and Stuttgart have experimented with shopping areas free from all automobiles, and the Schulstrasse in Stuttgart is particularly pleasant. Kassel has an interesting "stairway street" for shopping. Munich has a small system of arcades; so do Düsseldorf and Münster. These are comfortable, especially on rainy days of which there are a great many in Germany. Many cities such as Düsseldorf, Dortmund, and Stuttgart have handsome bridges to carry pedestrians over fast roads. All in all, thanks to these devices a pedestrian can have an easier time of it than in most American cities, but such facilities are not extensive enough anywhere. Moreover, the pedestrian islands for shoppers have been opposed by merchants just as they have in America, merchants with no sense of community and no sense, for that matter, of the realities for the shopper, of streets which carry vehicles but upon which he can never park anywhere near the shop. Once the car-free units are created, the merchants thrive, but the good examples seem incapable of stimulating enough imitation, just as Rockefeller Plaza has been much praised but rarely emulated even by the Rockefeller Center Corporation. So these devices are too few, and American planners will not find important novelties in Germany on this score or important ideas on how to win their victories at home.

Certainly as you look superficially at any of the new German city plans, you will tend to notice at once the system of radial and peripheral fast roads that are being proposed; but nowhere in plan or in execution will you see any disposition to make so much of these as to realize the dream of the megalomaniac road builder of Los Angeles who boasted that by 1970 every citizen would be living within two or three blocks of a freeway. As you look at the maps of such cities as Stuttgart or Essen, or especially as you walk around such cities, you will be depressed by the large number of areas given over to parking lots. These unseemly messy congeries of ugly vehicles seem to be everywhere and always full. They arose not as a consequence of urban taxes which is the American experience but because vacant land cleared of rubble was available for this use until construction could begin. Many interesting and imaginative garages are being built in the German downtowns, attached to department stores as in Cologne or Düsseldorf or standing alone as does the distinguished and comfortable Parkhaus in Frankfurt near the Opera;

166
Stuttgart. Die Schulstrasse.

but it is obvious that they are not keeping pace with the growth of the automobile population. Meanwhile the carparks are most unsightly, filling the Römerberg in Frankfurt, swallowing up the cathedral in Münster, defacing the market square in Bremen, making the market square in Freiburg almost unusable, and covering up Norbert Kricke's sculpture in front of the Mannesmann building in Düsseldorf to the point of absurdity. It is touch-and-go whether the garages, the German sense of order, and the high standards of public transportation will stem the tide. The Hauptbahnhof in Stuttgart is still a busy place, more than a sixth of Frankfurt's day workers come in daily by train, and the Berlin subway is a joy to ride. There are as yet no peripheral plasmoids to keep people out of the city, and proper control of land and speculative building may continue to keep them from becoming cancerous as they are here. There is much more hope in Germany that peripheral outlets for population growth will be provided in the German equivalent of the French *grands ensembles*, though I think in better form since there is already good German precedent for such developments in Zuffenhausen, Weissenhof, and the various prewar *siedlungen* of Berlin. The new ones such as Neue Vahr in Bremen are promising, though less gay and urban than Vällingby in Sweden and less bucolic than Täpiola in Finland; and there may be no single new German estate as pleasant and coherent as Roehampton. Traffic is less serious in Germany than here, despite the notorious defect of Germans behind the wheel, but unhappily this is probably nothing but a consequence of time lag.

Indeed, the automobile problem is never really solved. The example of Hanover is typical. Originally parking lots were planned for 6,000 to 7,000 cars. The demand has tripled. Although big free public parking lots exist in the center of town, an underground multistory parking lot for 340 cars

had to be built in front of the Opera. Parking buildings are to be built in the center of the city on land reserved for them. But the problem here as everywhere else is reminiscent of that of *The Sorcerer's Apprentice*.

This is the Achilles' heel of the German cities, and one can hardly exaggerate the vulnerability. The plain fact is that the private automobile and the daytime truck are rapidly killing the cities they have not already killed all over the world. They are murdering Tokyo, Teheran, and Istanbul as they have already murdered New York, London, and Paris. We all know it. But we do nothing.

The once elegant Place Stanislas in Nancy has become one great municipal parking lot. So has the Place Kléber in Strasbourg. The Champs Elysées is nothing but a *piste gazonnée* for automobiles rolling four deep down to the Concorde so that this boulevard is no longer elysian either for the boulevardier, the user of the café, or the elegant cocotte. The cars wheel incessantly around the Unknown Soldier at the Étoile. Things are at a standstill in the Strand most of the time, and if automobiles are repulsive when speeding dangerously by, they are even less attractive when standing still belching out carbon monoxide and smog-inducing exhaust. Automobiles have appropriated much of the lake front of Chicago, a good deal of the Embarcadero in San Francisco, both river banks of Manhattan Island; they have claimed one side of the Charles River Basin in Boston and are about to get the other side; they have cut Seattle in two, and separated the river front of St. Louis from the city as if by a wall. The story is everywhere the same. The Boston experience is typical, except that characteristically its traffic is a little slower than most. Three times in the winter of 1963–1964 the city traffic almost came to a full stop. Each time it was a Friday afternoon and very wet weather, but the atypical condition is irrelevant. Some people simply abandoned their cars in the streets, which of course made things worse. Every street was clogged, not merely the main exit avenues. It took four hours to accomplish a journey by automobile which might normally have required less than one. In the sober and frugal reappraisal of the cities' traffic problems, all anyone has been able to suggest is that another freeway be driven into the city and some more parking garages be built. Of course, all this does is aggravate the problem at the points of ingress and egress while contributing to that ultimate day when no one will come to the city at all or when all traffic stops and no one can get out.

Berlin, like other German cities, has not resisted the temptation to grasp at more and more roads and lots. The urban motorway scheme started in 1956 is designed to provide a little more than sixty miles of fast roads (it is about eight miles from West Wall to East Wall in Berlin at the waist). There will be a ring twenty-five miles long with full access control. It will not have grade crossings, nor will the most important intersections of the roads leading to the city. These roads form a design roughly resembling a ticktacktoe field, and the ring will divide the city into nine fairly even areas. The urban motorways, now partly completed, are to be three lanes wide each way and of course separate; when completed they will make the parts of the city they traverse look very much like Los Angeles.

If they go no further the city will still be inhabitable as a city (Los Angeles is inhabitable but not as a city). The hope of the Berlin planners is that their fine subway system will contribute to the containment; but more positive measures are going to be required in West Berlin and everywhere else.

When one looks back over just a few years of American urban experience, it is hard to avoid indignation. We know what is going on and do nothing.

We continue to subsidize the motor industry with great tax-supported highway systems while declining to make other means of transportation, especially the public ones, attractive enough to use. We do nothing whatever to inform motorists what their private journeys to the city really cost. We praise planned obsolescence. We continue to pamper merchants in the myth of the customer who drives right up to the store door and parks. The plain fact is that he drives past two or three times, then parks a mile or more away and walks back to the store or gives up. Yet every merchant resists, and so do hotel owners and other commercial interests, any effort to recapture any streets from the motorcar and to make them pleasant and safe for pedestrians—and we are afraid to do anything about their opposition, just as we do not enforce the parking laws we have. I know a distinguished Boston citizen who boasts that it is cheaper for him to park conveniently whatever the violation and pay the fines when caught than to pay for a garage every day. Last year it cost him 48 dollars.

In such circumstances a nice little footbridge (open to the elements of course) across a river of traffic, a closed street here and there, even a little greenery, seem absurdly insufficient. There are some principles that could be followed:

1. There are no inalienable rights to leave a private automobile anywhere except in designated parking areas.
2. If the car or the pedestrian must go underground, it is the car which must go.
3. If the car and the pedestrian are in competition for a river bank, or a view, the pedestrian should always be favored.
4. There is no necessity for a car (or even a truck) to be able to touch every building. It is easy enough to arrange superblocks at least a mile across, with a system of underground communica-

tions within which people can operate to shop and work and lounge without ever seeing, hearing, or smelling an automobile; and such areas should provide for walking in the sun and rain or being sheltered from them as one chooses, but not in tunnels, while the designs should be free from stairs that make the routes of cripples or of local goods too difficult. The Rows of Chester are still the prototype for most of this.

All these things and more are well enough known, and bits and pieces of solutions can be seen here and there, for example, Place Ville Marie in Montreal. Moreover, proposals such as Victor Gruen's for Fort Worth and Le Corbusier's more general and theoretical ones are available for study. Indeed, proposals have been provided for almost fifty years by Garnier in France and Corbett in the United States, and the Garden of the Palais Royal in Paris is a lot older still. The German rebuilding seems to take no account of this at all, resembling most of ours in its bow to the assumed foresight of merchants.

It is embarrassing for a citizen of the United States whose failures in urban planning and in general urbanity are among the most miserable to castigate the failures of another country; but we are talking here of Germany and not of the United States and the tone of the castigation is more one of sorrow than of anger. One feels that there is no real ultimate excuse for the damage done in America by the freeway builders. Nonetheless some of the German conditions might have been less restrictive, had they had a chance to look at us and be horrified. It is doubtful that many Germans would be heard to say that what was good for the Volkswagen company was *ipso facto* good for Germany. The vast areas of demolition opened up opportunities for better grouping so that important islands of peaceful commerce could not be dismissed by the scornful comment of a Texas banker who said he did not want to do business in a palm garden. Germans are better walkers than Americans and less fearful of inclement weather.

Despite all these possible advantages, there is very little design of enclosed places secure from the automobile in the new German planning, not even in most housing projects—certainly not in commercial and urban cultural space, both of which they could serve very well. In terms of what was possible, the little shopping areas of Essen and Stuttgart are trivial.

One example of what might have been and will not be is Ernst Reuter Platz in Berlin. This is now one of the most important intersections in Berlin where the Bismarckstrasse and the Strasse des 17 Juni cross the Otto-Suhr-Allee and the Hardenbergstrasse leading from Tegel to the Kaiser Wilhelm Gedächtniskirche, the Kurfürstendamm, and the principal shops and hotels. It is a focal point, and it was natural enough to develop it as a great traffic circle, lined with important commercial buildings. Indeed, the best commercial buildings in Berlin, at least for the moment, are here, including the twenty-two story Telefunken building by Paul Schwebes and Hans Schossberger, the highest building in Berlin (and as high as Berlin needs); the Osram House by Bernhard Hermkes; the building of the Faculty for Mining and Metallurgy by Willy Kreuer; the recent IBM building by Rolf Gutbrod, and so on. The buildings are in reasonable scale, and their designs not incompatible. It was also a pleasant but an insufficient idea to devote the large inside of the circle to a kind of garden plaza with grass and flowers and fountains. The street furniture is gentle, the flower boxes many and full of flowers in bloom, free of cigarette butts and empty plastic milk bottles.

Yet Ernst Reuter Platz offers no such serene composition as is provided by the Place des Vosges,

167

167
Berlin. Ernst Reuter Platz.

the Place Vendôme, the Place Stanislas, or even the more diverse Piazza San Marco in Venice, or the Piazza dei Signori in Verona—not even as much as was displayed by the original Rockefeller Center. The compositional effect is more like that of Mellon Square in Pittsburgh, though the open space is more generous.

There is not much reason for a passerby to move into the central green area, considering the effort required to cross the traffic or go down and up via a tunnel. When you get there, all you can do is sit in a shadeless place and look at some examples of contemporary commercial architecture while the automobiles roar round and round. Unfortunately, it is not even helped out much by such a fine piece of sculpture as Bernhard Heiliger's *Die Flamme,* a memorial sculpture for the famous mayor of West Berlin. In the end, of course, the volume of cars will equal that of the Étoile, and the experience of being in the center will not be happy even for those who take their sandwiches there from the nearby offices on sunny days. They can hardly go there in the rain since there is no shelter.

When all is said and done, the visual amenities of this Platz are primarily those from the air, from the windows of the buildings which front it, and from the automobiles which circle around it. This is all all right but not enough; and it is not enough because Ernst Reuter Platz was considered first and foremost as a highway.

The circle should have been girdled by the streets, of course; the buildings should have formed a wall between the traffic and the inner gardens which then could have been developed for the easy use of the occupants of the buildings and others who knew enough to go inside. This "Spanish" solution would have been more urbane for everyone except the motorist driving around the wall and for those who can judge the beauty of Berlin only on a half day's drive during which they never get out of a car. But the amenities of a city do not belong to such people. The Palais Royal Allée in Paris is not very impressive from outside but how charming and restful within. The "backs" of Cambridge, England are not available to the man on wheels. Urban pleasure areas need not be, either.

Or there was an alternate solution for Ernst Reuter Platz if the traffic circle had to be inside the buildings. It might have been depressed so that the central park covered it and went right to the buildings—this would have been putting the cars where they belong, underground in cities and above ground in the country. Or if the cost of depressing the street was too great or there were other technical difficulties, the main building entrances might have been put at the second floor and a great annular terrace built out from them to cover the traffic circle and offer a wide range of pleasures to the imagination. And if Berlin could not afford the annulus today, the requirement might have been made of all the new buildings that they be so designed as to provide for a second-floor entrance tomorrow. Much of our difficulty in raising our streets a story above the present grades and devoting the tunnels to the cars and the decks to the pedestrians is that the design and use of the existing buildings created yesterday make it almost impossible within any reasonable economy today or even tomorrow. Foresight might have entered into Ernst Reuter Platz if actual achievement had to be postponed.

But it did not, and so Ernst Reuter Platz is nothing but a fairly decent example on a presently comfortable radius of a quite conventional and indeed obsolete urban solution. It is, however, representative of the best that is to be observed in Germany right now. The little closed streets are of course better, but they and the neat pedestrian bridges of Düsseldorf are, as I have said, at once too little and too late. Indeed, the ultimate warning a visit to Germany should give to an American is the memory of what our urban life might have been if we had learned to keep the automobile in its place. For the Germans there is still some time. For us the hourglass is all but empty. But for cities which escape hostile sack or Diaspora there is still always the chance to turn the hourglass round again, either to accomplish something or idly to watch the sands trickle through once more.

Index